WHEN IT PAINS, IT ROARS
WHEN IT LAUGHS, IT SOARS

Reflections on some of life's little lessons
and other stories that are good for the heart

Charles P. Saunders

CHARLES P. SAUNDERS

TATTERSALL
PUBLISHING

Tattersall Publishing
P.O. Box 308194
Denton, Texas 76203-8194
www.tattersallpub.com

First Edition

Copyright © 1999 by Charles P. Saunders

All rights reserved. No part of this book may be reproduced or transmitted in any form or by any means, electronic or mechanical, including photocopying, recording or by any information storage andretrieval system, without the written permission of the publisher, except where permitted by law.

Printed in the United States of America

02 01 00 99   010   1 2 3 4 5

Cover Illustration by Crystal Wood

Library of Congress Catalog Card Number: 99-70933

ISBN 0-9640513-8-9

Preface

This book has been fermenting in the mash barrel of my mind for some time. For many years I have gathered various experiences, anecdotes and stories with the idea of stirring them together into a signature brew to share with others.

To make a perfect brew, among other ingredients you have to have the right blend of hops, malt, sugar and salt. No one of those should overpower the others. It should not leave a metallic, spoiled or acidic taste in the mouth. It has to be aged just right. It must have good clarity. And, of course, it must have just the right amount of head.

I have tried in this book to combine elements such as humor and sorrow, frivolity and seriousness, irreverence and reverence in just the right combination to offer you the finest possible handcrafted draught for the heart. The rest I leave to you. If you find that this little collection makes you chuckle, sigh or wince as you recall similar experiences in your own life, then this spirit will have achieved its intended result. Not every experience, anecdote or story offers a moral at its conclusion, though some do. Thank you for picking this up and imbibing it. Enjoy to the last drop.

Acknowledgments

This book was written in large part due to the loving support and encouragement of my wife, Sarah, who believed in me and said, "You can do it!"

I want to thank Si and Connie Dunn for their positive critical suggestions that were instrumental in shaping this work into respectable manuscript form. And a special "Thank you!" goes to Crystal Wood both for her keen editorial sensitivity and her insights that helped bring out the best of what I was trying to say as well as her discipline and hard work in guiding "When It Pains" through the publication process.

The responsibility, however, for the content of this book and the final form of the material in it is mine alone.

This book is lovingly dedicated
to Mom and Dad.
You taught me the most important lessons in life
through your words
and by your deeds.

Dear Jacqueline,
 I think you are
wonderful — hope you
enjoy this.
                Charlie

TABLE OF CONTENTS

Preface iii
Acknowledgments v

Part 1: Childhood Years
Electricity Is Nothing to Fool Around With 3
Childhood Fears 3
On Being Adopted 5
Third Grade "Death Penalty" 7
Déjà Vu 8
Seeds of Prejudice, Part 1: The Sowing 8
How to Tackle a Big Problem 9
The Hardest Stupidity to Bear is Always My Own ... 11
Stinky Feet and Romance Don't Mix 12
Perseverance Will Win Out 13
A Walkby in Arkansas Can be Hazardous 15

Chapter 2: Teen Years
When It Pains, It Roars 19
You Can Find Something to Like About Anyone 20
Mental Anguish vs. Pain and Suffering 22
Thank God for Braces 23
The Difference Between Profanity and Cussing 25
Seeds of Prejudice, Part 2: The Growing 26
Paper Doves Don't Die 27
A Change in Self-image Works Wonders 29
Fixing a Cheater 30
Seeds of Prejudice, Part 3: A Harvest of Grace 31
Paying for My Own Prank 33
Kissing at Church Camp 35

Chapter 3: College Years

Let's Join Hands for the Blessing 39
Mom and Moratorium 40
I Hope That's His Finger 41
Chemistry Professor Reduced to Tears 42
Definition of an Incentive 43
A Kangaroo Rat By Any Other Name 45
Guilt is the Heaviest Burden to Bear 46
"It Just Ain't Right to Say Grace Over Stolen Food" 48
Three Simple Secrets for Success in College 50
Memorable Quotes 50
A Cow Nose Best 51
How a Creme Puff Changed My Life 52
The Original Language of the Holy Spirit 53
No Reason to Wake Up 54
Law Professor Throws Down the Gauntlet 55

Chapter 4: Marriage, In-laws and Kids

P.B. Doesn't Stand for Peanut Butter 59
"Oh, God," Parts 1 and 2 59
Cows Do Big Jobs 60
A "Hunger Banquet"? 61
A Mosquito and a Willful Child 62
A big, biG, bIG, BIG Butt 63
If Santa Claus Is Not Real, What About God? 64
You Have to be Careful When You Handle a Gun 65
A Knothead and Nunchakus 66
The Lady Magnet and the Mustard Mustache 67
A Rock Up the Nose and Smashed "Jack-o-laters" 68

Chapter 5: Legal stories
Pantyhose and Final Argument 71
"If I'm Lyin', I'm Dyin'!" 72
The First Rule of Trial Law 72
Lawyer Bashing 73
Little Lady Lawyer from Dallas 75
The Definition of Coercive Contempt 76
The Volatile Judge 77
"Officer, I Don't Know This Guy" 77
Margaritas and a Blue Light Special 78

Chapter 6: Miscellaneous
The Problem Runs in the Family 81
Is God There If He Doesn't Seem to Answer Prayers? 81
"The Greatest Single Fee I Have Ever
   Received for My Professional Services" 84
"Feet Hurt! Boots Off!" 86
What Do You Get When You Cross A Garden
   Club With a Gentlemen's Club? 87
The Cockroach Letter 89
"Always Do What You Believe Is Right, Always!" 90
Ladies Found No Humor in Headline 90
Hair Pieces and Hell 91

Afterthought 93

PART 1:

CHILDHOOD YEARS

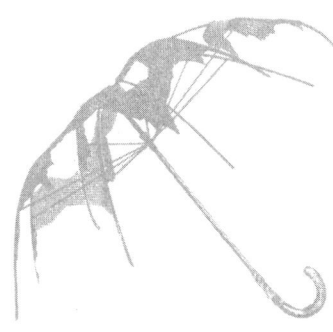

Electricity Is Nothing to Fool Around With

I must have been about six years old. We were at my grandma's house for the Christmas holidays. Grandma had a desk lamp that wouldn't work. I watched with great interest while Dad replaced the switch. As he finished, he looked up at me and said, "Charlie, you have to be real careful when you are working with electricity." To illustrate what he meant, he licked the end of his finger and flicked it toward the open socket. The lamp was plugged in. His aim, however, was off. Instead of grazing the edge, he jammed his finger directly into the socket. There was a flash of fire accompanied by a crackling sound and a large puff of smoke. I looked at Dad. His eyes were crossed and his hair was standing straight on end.

He made his point. When I grew up and became a lawyer I learned that is what is called demonstrative evidence. It sure made a believer out of me! From that time on, I knew beyond a reasonable doubt that electricity, like life, is nothing to fool around with.

Childhood Fears

My earliest childhood memory is of being afraid of the dark.

I remember waking in my crib in my room at night. It was dark. I was alone. And I was terrified. There were shapes in the dark, standing there watching me, waiting to tear into me if I got out of my bed. I couldn't move. I tried to call, "Mommy!" but my throat felt so tight; it wouldn't work. I tried to call, "Daddy!" I still could not make a sound. My terror grew as my whole body constricted and became so heavy; I could not move. I was afraid to move. I was soaked to my tiny bones with perspiration. My mind screamed, "*WOLVES!*" I am not sure if I knew exactly what "wolves" were, but I absolutely knew that was the word. They were waiting to get me, to rip into me if I got out of my bed. Finally, my throat hurting, I got out a small cry: "Mommy?" Daddy?" Nothing happened. I hollered again, but a little louder. The sound of my own voice piercing the darkness emboldened me, and soon I was shouting as loud as I could for my parents.

They came running and turned on the light. I think Dad picked me up. I was still screaming. I remember a terrifying feeling of not being able to stop gasping for air. Mom led the way and Dad followed, carrying me into the bathroom. He laid me down on my back on my bassinet. Mom wiped me with a cold, wet cloth. It felt good. Slowly, with a shudder, I was able to stop gulping air and to start breathing normally.

Throughout my childhood, I was plagued with fears both of the dark and of dogs, especially large ones. Eventually I learned to overcome them, though with considerable effort of will.

One time when I was home from college, Mom was reminiscing about old times. She told a story I had never heard before about a lady who was a popular baby-sitter whom my parents had hired several times to stay with me. Mom said that they quit using her after some of their friends had said that she would tell children there were lions, tigers, bears, or wolves in their rooms that would get them if they got out bed.

Wolves! It was as vivid as if lightning had flashed. Everything fell into place. I knew for certain that it had been the sitter who had told me there were wolves in my room—I had been afraid of the dark and dogs all those years because of some cruel, stupid woman. I was so relieved to understand why I had felt the way I had.

It seems to me now, though, that the lady actually did me a favor. I learned to recognize my fears. As I became older I decided that it was stupid to allow these fears to have control over me; I began to face them and scrutinize them. I realized that they were irrational. Whenever fear gripped me, I learned to make myself stay calm and to take several slow, deep breaths while I assessed the situation. For example, to deal with fear of the dark, I reminded myself that I had checked to make sure the outside doors were locked before I went to bed. I knew I had personally closed the closet and knew that nothing was in there. I asked myself was there any tangible thing I could identify that suggested that something or someone was actually there. There was not. I considered why I had waked up: maybe I had been having a bad dream. In time, the fear surfaced less often, and when it did it was much weaker. Eventually, I reached the point where I could say that I had overcome it.

On Being Adopted

"Mom! Mom!" I yelled as I came in the front door after school. "Guess what? Bobby is adopted." I did not know what that meant, but everyone in my second grade class was talking about it.

She said, "Charlie, come here, there is something I want to talk to you about." We sat down at the breakfast table and she asked me if I knew what that meant. Of course, I really didn't. She explained that sometimes people could not have children of their own and that sometimes there were children who did not have mommas and daddies. She continued that some of those people wanted to have children so much that they would take the children without parents and raise them as their own. She told me that several of my friends at school, including Bobby, were adopted. At last, she told me that she and Dad were some of those people and that they had adopted me and my sister. *I* was adopted!

There was much more to our discussion that I am omitting here. Out of thirty kids in my second grade class, six of us were adopted. Once I knew that, it did not seem like such a weird thing.

I didn't think much about being adopted after that until I was in ninth grade and we had to do a science project tracing family eye color. I realized I could not do the assignment. During my adolescence I grew quite a bit taller than my dad; people would sometimes ask him what happened. He would say, "He eats a lot."

However, it was not until my adult life that I connected a certain childhood fantasy I had with the fact that I was adopted. I had an aunt who used to say when I was small that I looked like Prince Charles. Maybe it was a result of that suggestion or one of the fairy tales that my parents read to me as a child, but I used to imagine that I was the secret son of a royal family. For some reason, they had to hide me to protect me from an evil witch or such as that. So they gave me to their trusted subjects, Charles and Mabel Saunders, to raise until it was safe for my "real" family to come for me one day. What was unique about my fantasy was that I had it long before that day my mom first told me that I was adopted.

I have since read accounts of other adoptees who have had similar fantasies. This is not to say that kids who are not adopted do not imagine the same things. Yet, the occurrence of such fantasies among adoptees is common.

Third Grade "Death Penalty"

In third grade, we studied the Wild West. As a part of learning about American Indians, we built a teepee in our classroom. We stood some tall poles together, wrapped butcher paper around them and painted Indian symbols on the teepee. Our teacher gave us strict instructions not to go inside it without her permission.

One day, I returned from noon recess to find that a bunch of kids were inside the teepee, horsing aroung. I marched over and, in my most superior-sounding voice, announced, "If Mrs. Bixby catches you in there, you're gonna get in trouble!" The teepee started to teeter. Suddenly, there was a loud "*Rrrrrrip!*" At that exact moment, in walked our teacher. Down crashed the teepee. She grabbed one kid who was crawling out by the ear and, with her other hand, pinched my cheeks together between her thumb and index finger. "I thought I told you not to go in there!" she shouted. I tried to tell her that I had not been in the teepee, but to no avail. Have you ever tried to talk while someone has your cheeks in a vise grip?

She never did believe me. Along with the true guilty parties, I received the third grade "death penalty"—no lunch recess for two weeks. We had to stay inside and work math problems. Ugh.

Though it did not scar me for life, I am still "purging" myself of that experience (as my college psychology professor used to say). I did, however, learn valuable lessons about justice. Every accused person deserves the chance to tell his or her side of the story. And, we should take the greatest care possible to see that we do not punish someone for something they did not do.

Déjà Vu

I believe I first encountered the term *déjà vu* when Crosby, Stills, Nash and Young released their hit song by that title. I learned what it meant the day I had an "already been there" experience when I was about eleven years old.

My parents took us on a trip from Texas up through Oklahoma, Kansas, Wyoming, Idaho, Oregon, Washington and Vancouver, B.C. Though I no longer remember the specific place and details, one experience is still clear. As we drove into one particular town, I asked Dad if we could stop at that malt shop they had there. He told me that I could not possibly know about such a shop, because we had never been there before. I insisted and told him what it looked like. I asked Dad and Mom if they remembered it. They told me it just wasn't possible.

As we entered the downtown area, I recognized the corner we were approaching. I told Dad that we were supposed to turn left right there. I *knew* it was just around that corner. I don't know why he chose to turn there, but he did. The ice cream shop was there, exactly as I had described it—I swear to God! Ever since, I have believed that there are lots of occurrences in our world that we do not know how to explain; we all should keep an open mind about such phenomena.

Seeds of Prejudice, Part 1: The Sowing

Fourth grade began for me in the fall of 1960. Kennedy and Nixon were campaigning for the presidency. Some people in our little "redneck" part of the world were saying that if Kennedy were elected, the Pope would run the country. I asked Mom and Dad who the Pope was. They said he was the head of all of the Catholic churches in the world. Dad rented office space from our family doctor (whom I later thought that the television series, "Marcus Welby, M.D." might well have been based upon), and our families were good friends. We were Protestants; they were Catholics. So, I figured that if the Catholic Church was made up of good, decent people like them, then the people who were against Kennedy because of that were ignorant. I did not really understand what prejudices were, but that would change in a few short years.

How to Tackle a Big Problem

My chief interest in the fall of 1960, when I was in fourth grade, was Peewee Football. My biggest challenge was to tackle this one kid who already stood six feet tall and weighed 160 pounds. In our scrimmages, we practiced against larger kids on a sixth grade team. This kid was bigger than any of the sixth graders, and I had already had my breath knocked out several times trying to tackle their fullback. How would I ever bring down Goliath?

Finally, we played the team with the giant. During the first half, when they had the ball, the other team would just grin at us every time they came up to the line of scrimmage. They had only one play—hand the ball to Goliath. We played six-man teams; it took all six of us to tackle him, and even then he would drag us several yards before going down. They scored each time they got the ball. The score was something like 34 to 13 at halftime.

Our coach had us huddle around him and told us we could beat those guys. He explained that, although that guy was huge, he was not coordinated; as long as we tried to tackle his body, he would just drag us like he had been doing. Then Coach let us in on a secret: If we tackled him around his ankles, he would fall over like a tree that had been chopped down.

I was ready the first time the other team got the ball in the second half. I steeled myself as I squared up directly in the lumbering hulk's path. Even though I believed Coach, I felt like my heart was going to beat right out of my chest. (I wonder if that is the way a bullfighter feels as he stands before a charging bull.) At the last second, I dove down in front of him and wrapped my arms around his ankles. He tried violently to jerk his foot free. I bit my lip but held on. Then he wobbled. Coach was right! I could hardly believe it; I had tackled the big ox all by myself.

In the length of perhaps a millisecond I had a flash of comprehension: "Oh my God, they yell 'Timber!' when a tree starts to fall to warn people to get out of the way." He was falling, and I was in his way. *Whoosh!* My breath was slammed from my lungs as all sixteen tons of him fell right on top of me. Then everything went black and someone was talking to me from far away. I hate getting my wind knocked out.

I no longer remember whether we won or lost that game. However, that day's lesson has stood me well ever since. The best way to tackle a problem is to cut it down at its weakest point. That is what effective business management does when dealing with a seemingly insurmountable problem. They break it down into its simplest parts and then solve them one by one. I have also found this approach works equally well when faced with personal trials in life.

The Hardest Stupidity to Bear Is Always My Own

My buddies and I used to have a place we called "the fort" in some woods at the end of the street. You had to crawl in under briars and then wind your way through a large stand of cane. There was a cleared out spot in the middle of the cane patch. From this hideout we would sally forth, imagining ourselves to be Sir Francis Marion, the Swamp Fox, and his men. We would attack the redcoat motorists by putting broken glass or nails in the street and then waiting from our position of cover to see what happened. When we were not engaging the British, we fought our own mock battles in which we vied with each other mainly to see who could do the best death fall. It was a great honor to be chosen the winner by the others.

One day in fifth grade, one of my fellow patriots accidentally stapled his finger. He fainted straight away. It was a perfect fall. In the Olympic death fall competition, he would have received scores of 10 across the board. I was so inspired that all I could think was that I, too, could fall like that if my finger got stapled.

You can see where this is going, can't you? It pains me to admit what happened next. Without a moment's thought, I took the stapler, stuck my finger in it and gave it a whack. I did not faint. I wished I had, though. God, did it hurt!

I made an amazing "duh"-scovery: It was stupid to staple my own finger! More importantly, I learned that I hated feeling stupid. What an incentive to think things through before acting. It's hard enough to put up with the stupidity of others, but the hardest stupidity to bear is always my own. Unfortunately, I have been reminded of this fact all too often since then, and each incident is a lesson in humility. I often wonder why the Lord insists that I take so many "refresher courses."

Stinky Feet and Romance Don't Mix

My fourth grade year had been awful. Constantly in trouble with our old battle-axe of a teacher, I had spent most of the year sitting in the dunce corner of our classroom (can you believe we actually had such a thing?) with the other "misfits." In later life, my parents told me that I had come very close to getting held back a year because the teacher told them I was "slow." Thank goodness Mom and Dad gave me the benefit of the doubt.

Then along came fifth grade. My new teacher, Miss Davis, took the time to work with me and encourage me. I liked her; she was young and pretty, and I worked hard to please her. Guess what? Before the fall term was over, I had caught up and was beginning to work above my grade level. I also was completely smitten by this new "goddess" of a teacher. (I just knew that I would marry her when I grew up.) I repeatedly begged my parents to invite her over for dinner, and they finally gave in and invited her. At long last my "cherished" was coming to my home.

Sighhhhh! Oh, how I still remember that night. I was outside playing when she arrived. I remember seeing her car in the driveway and rushing inside. She was sitting with my folks in our living room. I bounded in and gave each one a big hug, especially Miss Davis, then kicked off my sneakers and sat down by my mom.

Have you ever watched people's reactions as that first malodorous waft of foot odor invades their nostrils? Their noses crinkle up, nostrils flare out and eyes get that little involuntary blink. That was the look that crossed my beloved's face. She tried not to let on and smiled, except that her eyes twitched again.

Then my mom had the audacity to say, "Charlie, you need to go wash your feet." I just kept staring at Miss Davis and pretended that I did not hear. Again, only this time louder with a slight edge to her voice, my mom said, "Charlie! You need to go wash your feet." I stuck stubbornly to my guns. "No, I don't," I said, thinking *God, how could she say that in front of Miss Davis? Mom is going to ruin everything.* I knew she was right, but no way was I going to admit that in front of my teacher. Then, Dad spoke in that tone that brooked no argument on my part. "Charlie, your feet stink. Go wash them, *NOW!*"

Though my pride was dashed, I handled it stoically: I ran crying from the room.

I don't remember anything else about that evening, though I know she did stay through dinner. Strangely enough, when I saw her at school the next day, my crush on Miss Davis was over. I did, however, learn that stinky feet and romance don't mix.

On a deeper note, I sometimes wonder in what ways I have unintentionally traumatized my own children. I hope in my heart that this experience made me a more sensitive parent. (My kids would probably say that it only made me more sensitive to stinky feet!)

Perseverance Will Win Out

In sixth grade, I began taking piano lessons from a new teacher. She was much stricter than my prior teacher had been. I told my parents when they arranged for me to take lessons from her that I would not play in a recital, even though she required her students to play in recitals. However, from the beginning, my teacher made it clear that she expected me to change my mind. Eventually, I capitulated, though I don't remember how it happened. I only know that I felt trapped into playing.

The fateful recital day arrived. When it was finally my turn, I was a wreck. I began my piece. There were three movements to it. I got through the first part and started the second when . . . nothing. I went totally blank. I stared at the keys. I did the only thing I could think to do: I started the second movement again. The same thing happened! Try as I might, I could not think. I looked back, off the stage. There was no help there. So I started the second movement over once more. I was still blocked. I looked out at the audience. There was no help there either. I debated getting up and walking out but I could not bring myself to do that. I took a deep breath and started once more from the beginning. I made it past the block! There were some bobbles, but I got through it. I walked off the stage, out the back of the auditorium and then ran to our car where I sat and cried.

Eventually people began to come out. Several whom I knew and some I did not stopped to speak. Every one of them complimented me on my "perseverance." I did not know exactly what that word meant, but I was pretty sure it had something to do with sticking it out and not quitting.

I do not know the author, but the following quote is one of my favorites: "The difference between failure and success is not how many times you get knocked down, but how many times you get back up." Perseverance will win out.

There is another marvelous quote; this one is from President Calvin Coolidge. When I came across it years later, it reminded me of my experience at the recital. "Nothing in the world can take the place of persistence. Talent will not; nothing is more common than unsuccessful men with talent. Genius will not; unrewarded genius is almost a proverb. Education will not; the world is full of educated derelicts. Persistence and determination alone are omnipotent."

A Walkby in Arkansas Can Be Hazardous

Our family took a vacation to Lake Ouachita, Arkansas, one summer. It was about a six-hour drive and my sister, Gail, and I were restless and bickering. By the time we were well into Arkansas, Dad had warned us several times to "settle down." Finally, he said, "Next time I have to say something to you two, you are going to have to get out and walk."

Right, heh, I thought, with a mental chuckle.

It wasn't long until we were squabbling about something else. Suddenly the car began to slow and I looked up to see that Dad was pulling off onto the right shoulder of the highway. "Out!" he ordered, as soon as the car came to a stop. We climbed out and watched as he drove more than a quarter of a mile down the highway and then parked to wait on us. It was very hot. I think that was part of his strategy.

I told Gail that we should just keep on walking. She agreed. We planned to pass right on by when we reached the car.

As we approached the rear of the car, Dad got out, opened the door to the back seat and said, "All right, had enough?" I was in the lead. I said, "Nope, think I'll walk some more." On I marched. Unbeknownst to me, Gail had turned and climbed into the car. Next thing I knew, Dad was jerking me around by the arm with his right hand. His left hand already held his belt (how did he get it off so fast?). He bent me over and applied the belt persuasively to my butt. I decided that a walkby in Arkansas can be hazardous, especially when all you have to get by on is the seat of your pants.

PART 2:

TEEN YEARS

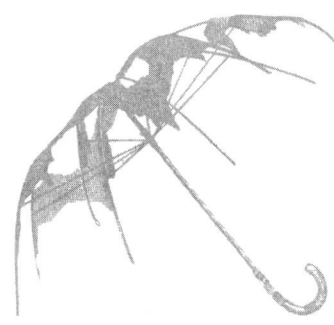

When It Pains, It Roars

Sometimes, kids misinterpret things that happen around them. These mistaken deductions can get lodged in their minds and affect them in odd ways as they grow older. I had one such experience that began when I was nine. I was in the fourth grade in the fall of 1960. I had a friend named Craig who was like an older brother to me. He was in seventh grade. His family visited us following the North Texas State University homecoming game that year. Craig and I tossed a football around in the yard. As he ran for a pass, he stubbed his toe on a brick alongside a flowerbed. Down he went, holding his foot. He was in pain and spent the rest of the time with ice on his toe. I learned later that an x-ray showed that his big toe was chipped.

As it turned out, I did not see Craig again until Christmas, because we lived about 150 miles apart. His family came to stay at his grandmother's house for the holidays. I was eager to see him. Then Mom explained to me that he was very sick and he might not look the same; he had something called leukemia. We went to visit their family. Craig was in pajamas and looked very thin and pale. His voice was weak. After about fifteen minutes, he tired of sitting up and had to go lie down. That was the last time I saw my friend.

One day when I came home from school a couple of months later, Mom met me at the door crying. I asked what was wrong and she told me she had something she needed to tell me. Craig had died. We cried together.

When I was in seventh grade, I went out for basketball. One day in practice, one of my teammates and I were both going after a loose ball and ran headlong into each other. We jammed our toes together. I could not run on that foot after that and by the end of practice I could hardly walk. The next day, I had my toe x-rayed. My doctor showed me the film. I could clearly see the bone chip in the joint of my big toe.

That evening, I did not feel like eating and went to bed early. Mom was concerned when I was still not eating the next night even though I did not feel sick. The following day when I came home from school, I was moping around. Mom asked me to sit down with her in the living room; it was the same spot where she had told me that Craig had died. We talked. She asked if anything was bothering me. Suddenly, I burst into tears. Sobbing, I told her I was going to die. She looked surprised and asked why I thought that. I explained how Craig had been in seventh grade when he chipped his toe, and he got sick and died from it. I, too, was in seventh grade and had chipped my toe just like he had; therefore, I was going to die. She hugged me saying, "Oh, no, honey, you're not going to die. Craig died from leukemia. That had nothing to do with chipping his toe." Boy, was I relieved.

From time to time, even to this day, that same old toe injury flares up. When it does, I remember my friend and the fun we had together. I still miss him.

You Can Find Something to Like About Anyone

When I was thirteen, I began working on a God and Country Award in Boy Scouts. Two other boys and I met for weekly study with our pastor, had assignments to work on during the week and worked at the church every Saturday. One of the boys was the minister's son, David. We did not like each other. I no longer remember what started the argument between us, but I do know we were in the church fellowship hall yelling, calling each other names and threatening to hit each other with claw hammers, when in walked his father and my mother. His dad told us that he could drop us from the God and Country program for such behavior. They made the two of us shake hands and apologize to each other; then we each went with our respective parent.

On the way home, Mom asked me what I liked about David.

"Nothing! I hate him," I retorted. She told me it was wrong to hate someone. She told me to name one thing I liked about him. I told her I did not like anything about him.

Then she taught me one of those basic, Golden Rule kind of lessons in life: I could find something I liked about him if I tried—and I had better try! I don't remember what it was, but I begrudgingly came up with something I liked about David. She was waiting for that. She said that if I could find one thing I liked about him I could find another. I told her another thing I "liked" off the top of my head. Then she used her closing argument on me: If I could find two things I liked about him, I could find three; and if I could find three, then four and so on. We might not end up being friends, but we would no longer be enemies.

Mom was right. During the months that followed as we worked on our God and Country Awards, David and I became friends.

I wish that someone could make the leaders of countries shake hands, say they are sorry and then have to find things they each like about the other.

Mental Anguish vs. Pain and Suffering

We had to take at least one semester of shop class in junior high school. I took it in seventh grade. Our shop teacher, Mr. Hollis, did not put up with nonsense or horseplay of any kind. Shop tools were dangerous and people could get hurt. It was well known that you did not want to cross him, because he kept a razor strap in his office that he used to give licks to anyone who got in trouble. He did not send boys to the office; he took care of the discipline himself.

One day when we came into the shop, Mr. Holllis' razor strap lay on a table top cut into pieces and then put together like a jigsaw puzzle. As the week progressed, he had each of us in his office for interrogation one by one (as well as each of the students in his other class). We never knew who squealed, but he soon found out who the culprits were. The next week, we observed Mr. Hollis personally supervising three of our classmates as they cut out, drilled holes in, sanded and then varnished their own paddles. On Friday, he had the entire class gather in the shop in viewing distance of his office.

One by one he had each boy bring in his paddle, hand it to him, then lean across his desk and grab the lip on the far side. He gave each boy three thunderous *thwacks* with his own paddle. It is no exaggeration to say he blistered their butts; we could see for ourselves when we changed into our gym clothes in P.E. I swear, to this day, I can still see the front legs of Mr. Hollis' desk lift off the ground with each lick. No one ever got out of line in his class again that year or during the next two, as long as we were there to warn the classes that followed.

In today's world, because a majority of people think it is abusive, corporal punishment no longer exists in our public schools. Based on my observations as an attorney, there is a growing juvenile problem in society. When I consider the disrespect that young people show toward their teachers and those in authority generally, the lack of physical discipline is, in my opinion, a great loss. I know that of those three boys, two of them probably changed directions in their lives because of that incident. More than that though, many boys were steered away from trouble by the example made of the ones who were paddled that day.

Watching our classmates prepare their own paddles that week created as much apprehension in the rest of us as it did in them. This is called vicarious experience. I did not realize it then, but I learned an important distinction that day. I did not have labels for that distinction until many years later when I took a course in law school called "Damages." I learned that there is a difference between pain and suffering on the one hand and mental anguish on the other hand. Mental anguish is what the guilty boys (and the rest of us) experienced up until the moment the paddle connected with their backsides, which caused pain and suffering—both then and for many days to follow. Mental anguish was even greater for the second one to get licks than for the first boy, because the second one got to see what was coming. The third boy's mental anguish was even more extreme. That was plain to see, since his face was ghostly pale by the time it was his turn to enter the shop teacher's office.

Thank God for Braces

Dad was a dentist. A dentist friend of his left his general dentistry practice to pursue specialty training to become an orthodontist. He returned to our town when I was in sixth grade. They agreed (unbeknownst to me) to put orthodontic bands on me without extracting any teeth. After nearly a year and a half, they took them off and I had teeth removed to make room for the shifting that was necessary to straighten my teeth. Needless to say, I was not happy to find out I had been a guinea pig. After several months of recovery from the extractions, they put new braces on my teeth, which I wore for three and a half more years.

I hated the braces with a passion. Beside the fact that I routinely took a ball or elbow in the mouth in sports, which shredded the inside of my lips, my kissing years were seriously delayed by these instruments of torture. If my folks had really wanted to threaten me when I was in trouble, all they would have had to say was, "You want us to have Dr. Penley tighten your bands? Then you better straighten up."

There actually was an experience that made me glad I had braces. One day a buddy of mine came up to me on the athletic field. He was angry at me because something I had told my mother about his girlfriend and him had gone from my mom to his mother. As a result, he had been grounded. There was shouting, shoving and then he suddenly took a swing at me with his fist. I guess it was a reflex, but my lips drew up as his fist came toward my mouth. I can still picture it as if the whole thing happened in slow motion. Maybe I momentarily had the gift of celerity. Anyway, there was a shock as his knuckles impacted my braces, followed by an ever-so-slight tug as he pulled his hand free—torn and bleeding. The fight was over. I had to pick small pieces of flesh off my braces, but I didn't mind. Neither did I mind the soreness in my teeth for the next few days. Thank God for braces!

WHEN IT PAINS, IT ROARS

The Difference Between Profanity and Cussing

I still smile when I recall one particular Boy Scout canoeing and camping trip. We were going down a stretch of the Brazos River between the Possum Kingdom dam and Worth Ranch about thirteen miles downriver. Several of our dads went along, including a man whom I will call Mr. Smith, the father of one of my best friends. As a kid, I had often been a guest in his home. My dad and I had gone dove hunting with him and his sons several times. I had never heard Mr. Smith utter a curse word in all those years.

At the end of the afternoon, we came to an island and decided to make camp there for the night. Mr. Smith was next to me. It was dark. Everyone had quit talking. You could hear all the night sounds. I heard him say in a hushed voice, "What was that?" Suddenly there was a thrashing noise accompanied by a loud, deep-throated basso *"rrrrrraaahhhhck,"* immediately followed by a wet, slapping sound like a raw steak had been dropped on the kitchen floor. Something had hopped onto the foot of his sleeping bag and he reacted by trying to kick it off. A very startled bullfrog croaked and leaped, smacking belly down on the face of an even more startled Mr. Smith. "Goddammit! Frog!" he blurted out. I burst into laughter as did others who were still awake.

That day I learned the difference between the vulgar use of profanity and cussing. Cussing captures a heightened emotional state with a purity and singularity of expression that plain, old habitual swearing could never achieve. Cussing leaves the speaker unsullied by his use of the curse words, where base vulgarity tarnishes and diminishes the user. Mr. Smith's speech certainly was not elevated to the level of the sublime; it did not even reach a level that would be considered inspired; but, it was most definitely expressive!

Seeds of Prejudice, Part 2: The Growing

I vividly remember exactly where I was when I learned that President Kennedy had been shot. As momentous as the assassination was, something much more important in my life occurred that same winter. I learned that I was a racist.

I attended a public junior high that was actually located on the North Texas State University campus. NTSU was integrated but the Denton public schools were not. It snowed one day while we were at school. By the time we got out of basketball practice after school, there was a blanket of snow on the ground about four inches thick. We were having a grand time. We were engaged in an all-out snowball fight on the football field when something happened. It was ugly; I still feel ashamed when I recall the incident.

There was a sharp incline at the south end of our field that descended about twenty feet to the sidewalk and street below. Suddenly, there were shouts of "Nigger!" and snowballs whizzing downhill. I ran to see. A girl was walking past trying to keep her balance on the slippery sidewalk. She was carrying a notebook and some books in her arms; she had raised them up to shield her face from the barrage of frozen missiles. I threw one snowball and yelled the N-word, my voice tinged with ... hatred?

As I drew back my arm for another attack, someone grabbed my wrist and jerked me around. I stared into Danny's eyes. He had been one of my friends since kindergarten and was probably the best athlete in our class. He said, "How would you feel if you were walking through an all-Negro neighborhood and a bunch of them started throwing snowballs at you and shouting, 'Whitey'?"

Instantly I knew the terror she felt.

The snowball fell from my hand and I joined him in telling the others to stop. That day, I took a bite of the fruit from the tree of the knowledge of good and evil. I shed my first racist skin on that snowy winter's day. It was a chilly awakening. As surely as Adam knew that he was naked before God, I knew that something ugly in my own soul had been laid bare. I could never go back to the garden of smugness again.

(I don't think I ever said it, but "Thanks, Danny!")

When I graduated from high school, a dentist friend of my dad's gave me a card. It bore the following quote from William Shakespeare: "To thine own self be true, and it shall follow as the night the day that thou canst not be false to any [one]." The path leading to self-honesty is perhaps the most difficult task we have as human beings. It certainly has been for me. How can we truly love others as ourselves until we first can be truly honest with ourselves?

Paper Doves Don't Die

Dad got me my first shotgun when I was ten. It was a J.C. Higgins (J.C. Penney's brand) 20-gauge, breech-action, single-shot. He took me on a dove-hunting trip. We camped with about fifty to sixty hunters on a farm near Woodson, Texas. It was dry, West Texas, 100-plus-degree weather. Scrub and mesquite trees surrounded fields growing various maize and grains. It may not have looked too inviting except to an occasional rattlesnake, jackrabbit or buzzard, but it was a hunter's paradise come the first of September, the traditional opening of the hunting season for mourning dove. Well, the hunting part was paradise. I suspect the only way the men could have looked on our physical surroundings as anything more than inhospitable was with the aid of the copious quantities of beer they consumed.

Anyway, it was not legal to begin hunting until noon. There were probably eight to ten kids there. My best friend Bob and I were full of excited energy; I'm sure we must have driven our dads crazy asking if it was time to start hunting yet. It was a quarter to noon. Finally, one of the men came up to the two of us and said, "Boys, I think I saw one fly into that tree there down the fence row." "But it's not time yet," we answered in unison. He said, "I think it's all right; it's close enough to time." We glanced anxiously in the direction of our dads. They nodded. We got our guns, loaded them and began cautiously to approach the tree. We were crouched over from the waist as though that would help keep the dove from seeing us.

It was only about 50 yards away but it took us awhile because we crept so slowly. Finally, we were directly in front of the tree. We froze. We could hear the man calling softly, "In there, right in front of you."

We both saw the dove at the same time; it was just sitting there.

We raised our guns slowly, aimed, counted—*BLAM!* Nothing happened. The bird just sat there. We whispered to one another:

"Didya hit 'im?"

"Dunno."

"Let's try again."

"Okay."

We aimed, counted and fired again. The dove remained still.

We crouched over and inched forward. It did not move. We raised up straight. It still did not move. A couple more steps forward. It was then that the hoots, hollers and laughs began. About the same time we could see bits of the paper dove blown all over the branch. One of the men that already had a pretty good start on some beer hollered, "Is it dead, boys?" and then broke into loud heehawing. We really didn't see the humor in it.

The prank was soon forgotten as the real hunting began. That night and the next, we had great feasts on fried doves and hush puppies. It was customary when we broke camp to give the farmer whose land we were leasing a couple dozen dove. The host of the hunt asked Dad if he would take care of this gratuity. He generously complied. As we headed home, not from any selfishness but just because he liked eating dove so well, Dad lamented, "Charlie, I really hated giving those birds to old Mr. Harris." I replied, "It's okay, Dad, I ate thirteen for dinner last night." He got a kick out of that and has often reminded me of it through the years.

A Change in Self-image Works Wonders

The summer between eighth and ninth grades, I attended a summer church camp in East Texas. We camped outdoors in the piney woods, cooked over campfires and held Bible study and discussions around the camp table at night. I noticed that the most popular guy ended up getting the most popular girl as his girlfriend. I thought about my observations at camp and came to a conclusion that there were certain things he did that made him popular.

I determined that I was going to become somebody different when I went to camp the next year. I would be with all new campers so no one knew me from the prior year. I noticed that that guy had been friendly to everyone, no exceptions; he knew everyone's name and greeted each person he encountered by his or her name. He was always cheerful. And he volunteered for every task that came up in camp. When he finished his chore, he joined in helping anyone else who was not finished with his or her chore. So, I became that guy. It worked! Everyone related to me the same way they had him to him. And I got the girl I wanted at camp to be my girlfriend.

I learned a happy truth. A change in self-image works wonders. I can change the way people respond to me by changing my self-image.

I also learned it is much harder to be a different person around the people who had known me for a long time back home. Most continue to see you the way that is already fixed in their minds. But I liked myself better when I was that new person, so some of the changes remained. To this day, I try to make a point to greet people and use their names if I recall them. Volunteering is still a great way to meet people and make friends. I continually see examples of these lessons demonstrated in our communtiy in the people who gladly give their time to worthwhile causes.

Fixing a Cheater

In my high school biology class, I used to sit next to this kid, Pat, who was the school bull-riding champion in FFA (Future Farmers of America). I guess it goes to say, he was a tough guy—not the brightest, but tough. He told me I had better let him copy off my exam or he would kick my butt. He also warned me not to tell our teacher, Mrs. McCauley. This bothered me greatly. I realized lots of kids (for that matter, adults, too) saw nothing wrong with cheating. I sweated it, though. I did not want to get an "F" if the teacher caught us. I devised a plan.

For our first test, I studied extra hard. When we started the exam, I took a minute to look it over. There were matching problems, true/false questions and multiple choice. Pat reached across the aisle and punched me to let me know I had better get started. So, I put my head down and began. I read each part carefully so I would remember it when I came back to it later. I then proceeded to mark the answers wrong. I did not realize it since Pat sat just back to my left, but he apparently answered some of the problems on his own and looked at my paper for the ones he wasn't sure of.

I paused and saw Mrs. McCauley watching us. As I think about it now, she probably already knew to watch him. Anyway, when he was finished, he turned in his paper and left so he would have time to go have a smoke before the next class. I then immediately erased all my answers and put down my real answers; I only had about ten minutes to finish. When I turned in my exam, I felt as though Mrs. McCauley was staring a hole through me. I looked her in the eye and said, "I can't say anything; just trust me."

When our test papers were returned to us, I made something like a 94. Pat made something like a 55. He just kept looking at his exam, looking over at mine and scratching his head. I do clearly remember the smile Mrs. McCauley gave me as she handed me my paper. Nothing ever was spoken between us about it; but, I know she knew. I don't know if Pat ever figured it out or not, but he never told me to let him copy off of my paper again.

It is very satisfying fixing a cheater.

Seeds of Prejudice, Part 3: A Harvest of Grace

At the end of our sophomore year, our school district integrated the Denton school system by closing the separate black high school. All of the students attended one high school starting in the fall of 1967. I met several of the guys from the other school prior to our schools actually being combined when we had a joint spring training for football. I thought I had dealt with my prejudice and was proud of it.

Then, the summer of 1968, I attended Texas Boys State along with several other boys from Denton. We all rode together to Austin, where it was held. One of the delegates was Shelton, an African-American who was one of the most popular guys in my class. I had first met him in the joint football spring training. We had a group discussion all of the way to Austin. One of the topics was racism. Shelton told us that the Klan was present in our hometown. Several of us did not believe that they were around any more. He said that we were naïve, and that they were still very much present. He said his parents would not allow him to stay in one of our homes because they felt that he (and we) would not be safe from the Klan.

At my first opportunity, I was quick to say that I did not think I was prejudiced. Later, the conversation had shifted to girls. Shelton mentioned his girlfriend's name. I said, "Is that who you go with? Wow, she's cute for a black girl."

Jimmy, the guy driving, said, "Charlie, do you realize what you just said? You're prejudiced."

"What?" I asked in a shocked tone. One of the others guys jumped in and said, "Yeah, you said 'for a black girl.' Why didn't you just say, 'She's really cute' without adding 'for a black girl'?" I was stunned.

I don't know if the other guys heard it or not—the deflating of my pride—but I did. To me, it could not have been louder than if someone had just run over a basketball with a steamroller. I shed my second skin of prejudice that day in that car. All I could say to Shelton was "I'm sorry, I didn't realize." He seemed to accept that response. There was no anger, no judgment. To his credit, I could never detect any change in his attitude toward me.

This is one of the most genuine examples of grace I personally have ever experienced. The only way I know that the differences that separate people can truly be overcome is by applying this kind of grace in our relationships with each other. We are all fallible human beings.

Racism is insidious. Since that day in the car on the way to Boys State, I have been unwilling to allow myself to develop a false sense of pride like I did before. As a hopefully exaggerated reminder, I can picture myself standing up at an imaginary RA (Racists Anonymous) meeting and proclaiming, "Hi, my name is Charles; I'm a racist." I was raised by good Christian parents and in a community with a seemingly benign attitude toward race. They truly did not espouse hate. These reflections are not meant to judge anyone other than myself; each of us must look into our own heart and deal with what we find there.

It may be thirty years too late, but I still want to say, "Thanks, Shelton, for having the grace to allow me to grow and change."

Paying For My Own Prank

It was high school speech class. I decided to pull a prank on a friend. The key to its success was setting it up innocently with a kind of take-it-or-leave-it offer that overcomes the person's natural suspicions. So that it would not be too good to be true, I only offered to bet my friend a Coke. The bet was as follows: I would hold a number two lead pencil in my fist with the point standing straight up and the eraser braced firmly against the desk top. The pencil was sharpened to pinpoint size. I bet him that he could not break the lead by taking his speech textbook and hitting the pencil point with the flat side of the book. I explained that it was a law of physics that if he brought the book straight down on the lead it would resist the blow and not crumble.

He thought about it and took the bait. He knew there was no way that lead wouldn't break. Our teacher walked into the back of our classroom unnoticed by those gathered around intently watching the challenge. My buddy (I might add, one of the strongest guys on our high school football team) picked up his textbook, raised it over his head and slammed it down extra hard to make sure the lead broke. The lead shattered (which was what it was supposed to do) as the pencil tip was driven all the way through the entire book. Roars of laughter broke out around us. My friend stared in shock at his speech book, and then angrily at me. At that moment it occurred to me that maybe it was not such a good idea to have pulled this trick on the strongest guy on the football team. But he was too amazed to be truly angry. "Look at my book!" he said. "I know," was all I could say before bursting into laughter again. At that point our teacher pushed through the crowd, saw the impaled book and said, "You boys are coming with me." Off we went to the principal, who lectured us and told me I would have to pay for the book (which seemed like a bargain compared to getting licks with a paddle from our principal).

It has been my experience that I usually end up being the one to pay for my pranks.

Ahhh, how I wish the story ended there. But, alas, it has a sequel that bears telling. I was not satisfied with my lesson from the first time I pulled this prank. No, I decided to repeat it one more time in college.

I went upstairs to the dorm room of a friend named Steve. The setup went smooth as could be. He bought the whole thing. He picked up a book off of his desk and, *Wham!*, drove the pencil almost the entire way through the thick textbook. I laughed with great hilarity. He looked at the book dumbfounded for and instant and then broke into uproarious laughter— so uproarious that I quickly stopped my own heehawing and asked him what was so funny. "Oh, by the way," Steve said, as he held the book out to me, "I meant to tell you, but I borrowed your psychology book from your room while you were gone." He had driven the pencil through MY book!

Needless to say, I was reminded of the whole incident every time I studied for that class the rest of the semester. Steve had the audacity to ask me to buy him the Coke because he had successfully smashed the pencil lead. The nerve of some people.

Kissing at Church Camp

I think I was slow in my experiences with girls. The first time I really kissed was my senior year of high school. That was the year I fell in love with the girl I would later marry. However, we were broken up for awhile after graduation (the summer of 1969). I attended a Presbyterian church camp called Mo Ranch that summer, located near Ingram, Texas, in the beautiful Hill Country along the Guadalupe River.

That week of camp, I had the experience of meeting a cute girl named Karen; I developed one of those summer camp crushes on her. There was another girl, DeDe (also very cute), who seemed to have a crush on me. The last night of camp, there was a chaperoned dance. I asked Karen to be my date and she accepted. Later, while I was talking to DeDe, I asked if she was going to the dance and she said she was. Well, when I got there, both girls were there. The problem was DeDe had taken my question as an invitation for her to be my date.

A normal guy would have told DeDe he was sorry, but he was there with someone else. Not I. Nope, I did a stupid thing. I took her upstairs (it was a split-level arrangement) and kept Karen downstairs. I used various artifices to leave one while I went and danced with the other. I would tell them I was going for sodas, going to the restroom or whatever I could think of. Of course, it did not work. Karen came looking for me while I was dancing with DeDe. She was understandably upset and told me so. That was the last I saw of her for the evening.

Well, what was a young stud to do, right? I acted like I did not know what that was about when DeDe asked and went right on with her like she was the one I wanted to be with; but, inside, she wasn't. When the dance was over, we had only a short time left to go to our respective dorms before our curfew. I walked DeDe to the girls' dorm. Across the way I saw Karen with a guy (whom I recognized as always having had a group of girls gathered around him at camp while he played a guitar). I really had a sinking feeling in the pit of my stomach seeing the two of them together.

Anyway, everyone looked a little nervous. I guess no one wanted to be the one to make the first move. Then something really cool happened. The camp director walked up about that time and said, "All right, on the count of three, everyone kiss good night: one, two, three." Boy, was that the way to cut through all the anxiety about what would happen if I tried to kiss her. Thus, we all kissed our dates.

There is an odd quirk to this story. I began college that fall at Austin College, a small, Presbyterian liberal arts college. I ran into Karen, who was enrolled there. She was friendly but not interested in me. I became acquainted with a guy named Joe and we became fraternity brothers. At some point, I told him my story about that last night at camp. When I came to the part where the camp director came up, Joe finished the story for me by quoting what the director had said. He had been there; he was the guitar player! He later became my best man when I got married. Still later on, Joe worked as a minister in training under the man who had been our camp director. How's that for a small world?

PART 3:

COLLEGE YEARS

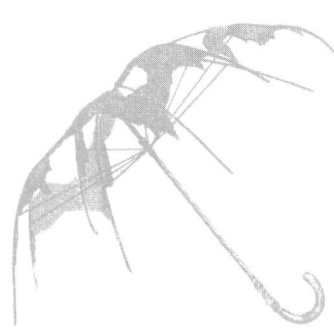

Let's Join Hands for the Blessing

I attended that same church camp with a fellow named Jim. We had met at a different camp a prior summer and hit it off. When we learned that we were both going to be attending the same college in the fall, we decided to see if we could room together. Each of us contacted the school's housing department with our request. We found out about two weeks before college that we had been assigned to the same room. So I went to his home in Dallas to visit him and to meet his parents. When I shook hands with his father, I noticed that he had no left arm.

Jim and I went to Six Flags Over Texas for the day with a couple of girls he knew. I spent the night at his home and attended church with his family the next day. After the service, we returned to their home where I joined them for their Sunday meal before I headed home. We sat around their formal dining table. His parents sat at either end, and Jim and I across from each other. His mother was to my left and his father to my right. His dad said, "All right, let's all join hands for the blessing." Without thinking about it, I held out my right hand to empty space. That was the side of his father's missing arm. I felt my face flush with that heated feeling I hate.

They all burst into laughter and told me it was a standard joke they pulled on guests the first time someone joined them for a meal.

It hasn't come up again that I can think of, but I still do an arm check when I sit down next to someone for a meal.

Mom and Moratorium

Vietnam was a major subject on everyone's mind the fall of 1969 when I started college. I remember going home from school for a weekend visit. I wore a black armband. My folks flipped out when they saw it. They wanted to know if I was a member of the SDS (Students for a Democratic Society), an activist group against the war that staged many rallies on university campuses around the country. It seemed there was some clash between student protest groups and the authorities almost nightly on the television news. I told my parents that students all over were wearing armbands in observance of a moratorium. It was a symbol of mourning for all lives sacrificed by Americans in all of the military conflicts in our country's history, including Vietnam.

They would not leave me alone about the armband. Mom said that she wished I would not wear it while I was at home. I told her to look at me because what I was about to say was important. She did. I said, "I want you to look me in the eye. Now tell me you believe so strongly in what our country is doing in Vietnam that you would be proud if I were killed serving my country there and sent home to you in a wooden box."

There was a potent silence. Then, still looking me in the eye, she said, "No, I couldn't say that." That was the last time either of my parents said anything to me about the armband. The thought of bodies in wooden boxes has a way of bringing war home to people, at least where it concerns their loved ones.

I Hope That's His Finger

Austin College had a different academic calendar. The fall term ended before Christmas. Then there was a concentrated, month-long course during January which was called "Jan. Term." This was followed by the spring semester, which was over at the end of May. My first Jan. Term I signed up for a course called "The Interrelation of Religion and Personality." We only had to read eleven books! The class met each day for two hours for lectures and discussion on our readings. We also had to write a report on each book. It was heavy stuff. We went to Denny's restaurant every night and sat at a table drinking coffee because refills were free, usually reading until 3:00 or 4:00 in the morning.

The class was taught by a professor of religion whom I shall call Dr. Rose. Dr. Rose always wore a short-sleeve dress shirt with a bow tie, a sport coat with elbow patches, slacks and Hush Puppies. He was widely known for his eccentric mannerisms. For example, he would lean back in his chair while he was lecturing and balance precariously. He fell over more than once in class. At other times, he would take his pocket watch out of its pocket while he was lecturing and twirl it around his finger, first to the right until it wound tight; then, he reversed the direction, unwinding it, and then wrapping it around his finger in the opposite direction. He would do this back and forth. Another of his nervous habits was to take off his half glasses, fold them up and put them in his coat pocket; a moment later he would take them out, unfold them and put them back on. He would repeat this all the way through his lecture.

Dr. Rose's funniest quirk was to tuck his fingers down inside the waistband of his trousers with his thumbs hooked outside over his belt. One day he was doing this while his fly was down. He was not aware of it but he was wiggling his fingers out of his fly.

Everyone was stifling laughs while poking the person next to them and pointing to the daring digits. One girl blurted out, "Oh, my God, look!" and pointed. This was enough to draw his attention first to her and then along the line of her extended finger back to his fly where he saw his own fingers wiggling out.

He stood there for a moment and just stared. Finally, Dr. Rose cleared his throat, raised his eyes until he was peering over his half-focals and said, "Class dismissed." He then turned his back to the class and adjusted his zipper.

Chemistry Professor Reduced to Tears

Dr. Edwards, who was perhaps the most interesting professor I ever had, taught freshman chemistry. He truly loved teaching and conveyed his enthusiasm to us. He was also a brilliant man, having worked at Oakridge, Tennessee, during the days they were in the race with White Sands to develop an atomic weapon. He would get so wound up in a lecture that, when the blackboard was full, he would continue writing on the wall. Sometimes it was hard to take notes because I would get so spellbound by his presentation that I would forget to write. He was one of the most admired and respected members of the faculty.

One day, Dr. Edwards was in the middle of a lecture when a guy in our class stood up, slammed his book closed and then clapped his notebook shut. He threw his book down on his notebook and grabbed both up off the desk. He shouted, "I've had enough of this crap!" and stormed out of the classroom.

Not a soul dared even exhale. It was absolutely silent for a long moment. Then, Dr. Edwards practically spit as he burst into laughter.

He was barely able to say, "You should see your faces!" before breaking into another paroxysm of belly laughter. We were in utter shock. By this time, the professor was laughing so hard, he had tears streaming down his face. In between spasms of laughing he said, "We ... set that up ... before class." He was contagious; soon the whole class was drawn into uproarious laughter. Once he finally caught his breath enough, Dr. Edwards explained that the guy had informed him that he needed to leave class early, and Dr. Edwards had asked the guy to help him pull a joke on the class.

Definition of an Incentive

I worked summers after each of my first two years of college painting dormitory rooms at the University of North Texas (formerly North Texas State University). The pay was $2.25 an hour, which was good compared to minimum wage at $1.65 an hour. We worked in pairs. Each pair would go into a room and prep it, which meant taking switch and outlet covers off, taping paper around the baseboards and putting down drop cloths. One of us then painted the room's walls with a roller while the other used a brush to do closet woodwork, door frames and to trim along the top of the walls up to the ceiling. When we were finished, we had to clean up the room and replace the covers.

The teams settled into a pace of finishing four rooms per eight-hour day. After about the third week, our foreman called the whole crew together for a meeting. He said we needed to get more rooms done to finish the buildings that were scheduled for painting during the summer. The next few days we still averaged four rooms per eight hours. On Friday, he called us in and told us that if we got four rooms finished and they passed inspection, we could go home with eight hours' pay. The slowest team finished in about five and a half hours.

On Monday, our foreman informed us that if we could finish four rooms in five and a half hours, then we should be able to complete five in eight. The rest of that week the pace continued at four rooms per eight hours. On Friday, the boss again told us that if we finished four rooms and they passed inspection, we would again get to go home with eight hours' pay. All of the teams finished by no more than five and a half hours.

Monday morning, the foreman called another meeting. He was exasperated with us and asked what the deal was. One of the guys on the paint crew, who was a Vietnam veteran attending college on the GI Bill, said, "Well, Boss, a fast painter gets paid two dollars and twenty-five cents and hour and a slow one gets paid two and a quarter." In other words, there was no incentive for the faster, better painters to outperform the slower ones.

The foreman was so close to figuring it out that I still cannot believe he never did get what he wanted. Each team was turning out 20 rooms a week. By offering to pay us for 40 hours if we finished 25 rooms per week and they passed inspection, he could have increased our production by 25 percent. But he never made that intuitive leap.

That summer I learned what an incentive is. If more businesspeople took the time to truly understand this principle, they could significantly increase the productivity of their employees. Zig Ziglar made a fortune as a motivational speaker. Amidst the mass of practical wisdom he shared when he spoke to a crowd was always a core message. "You can have anything you want if you help enough other people get what they want." That is exactly how an incentive works; if a businessperson offers his or her employees something they really want, they will give the businessperson the desired level of performance.

WHEN IT PAINS, IT ROARS

A Kangaroo Rat By Any Other Name

Each year during the Jan. Term at our college, a biology professor named Dr. Pearce would take a small group of students on an extended field trip lasting a couple of weeks. The course was called "Desert Biology." The class would study birds with binoculars, trap small game in cages and observe the changes in plant growth as they travelled through the different ecological zones from West Texas to New Mexico and then into Arizona. One of the highlights of the trip was capturing kangaroo rats and bringing them back. Some of the animals remained in the laboratory for studies that Dr. Pearce was conducting regarding how they produce water from their food. Each student who wanted to got to take a couple of kangaroo rats home to keep as pets.

At the beginning of our sophomore year, there was one extremely naïve freshman named Preston. He saw a kangaroo rat that one of my friends had in a cage in his room. Several of us were sitting around when he asked what it was. On an impulse one of the guys said, "It's called a dildo."

Preston looked at him and said, "A what?" The guy repeated it for him. He said, "Hmmm, I've never heard of one of those before." Another guy in the room pounced on the opportunity to get in on the joke and told him facts about "dildos" and how they got them on the desert biology trip.

Preston had been around long enough to be just a bit suspicious. I told him that if he did not believe us, he could go over to the biology lab and see them for himself. Someone told him to ask Dr. Pearce. Off Preston went to the biology lab.

Now Dr. Pearce was also our fraternity faculty sponsor, so we called the lab. We happened to get him on the phone and explained the whole scenario. About half and hour later, Preston showed back up and said that the "dildos" were really cool. Dr. Pearce had told him all about them and showed him the ones he had in the laboratory. Preston wanted to know how he could get one. One of the other guys in the room said he thought that some of the students had sold their animals to the pet store in the nearby mall. Someone else chimed in, "Yeah, maybe they still have some."

Preston wanted to go get one right then. Someone agreed to drive and off he went with a carload of his pals along for the ride. At the pet store, a nice little lady working behind the counter asked Preston if she could help him. He said, "Yes, ma'am, I would like to buy a dildo."

She seemed to look right through him and said "A what?"

He repeated, "I would like to buy a dildo."

She said in a rather shrill, sharp voice: "I suppose you think you're funny coming in here and asking me that. How dare you!"

He knew something was wrong then; or, perhaps our inadequate attempts at stifling our snickers gave it away. Whatever the case, she ordered us out of her store and told us not to come back. We went straight to the lab to report the outcome to Dr. Pearce, and he joined us in a hearty laugh upon hearing the tale. I believe none of us ever considered how the lady sales clerk felt as an innocent victim of our prank.

Guilt is the Heaviest Burden to Bear

I dropped out of college during my junior year, got a job and married my high school sweetheart, Barbie. I worked as a Pizza Hut manager while she finished her nursing degree at Texas Woman's University. We lived in Dallas during her senior year. After she

WHEN IT PAINS, IT ROARS

graduated, we moved back to our hometown of Denton just north of Dallas. She began work as an R.N., and I enrolled in college that fall. However, we soon learned we were expecting our first child. So I took the only job I could find working at a local hamburger and barbecue restaurant as a manager trainee.

One day at noon, a man in a wheelchair came in. After he ate lunch, he struck up a conversation with another employee and me. He began what I call his testimony. He related how he had grown up in Mississippi and had hated "niggers." He said that he had been a member of the Klan and had done some pretty awful things he was not proud of, though he did not say what they were – and we did not ask. He then said he was trying to make up for the wrong things he had done by stopping everywhere he went and telling people his story.

He had been drafted and had gone to Vietnam. They had been under attack and a grenade landed in his foxhole. He said there were four men in it. One of the other soldiers dove on top of the grenade. It killed him instantly, but his action saved the lives of the other three. The man said, "He was black; he gave his life up to save mine." His voice began to break as he continued, "After all the hateful things I had done and even the hateful things I had said to him, he sacrificed his life to save mine and the other guys in the hole." The man went on to say he hoped that by telling his story he might turn others from their hatred of black people.

I never saw the man again. I do hope his mission was successful, and when I think about him I pray for him. Guilt is the heaviest burden to bear.

"It Just Ain't Right to Say Grace Over Stolen Food"

I did something I was not proud of when I worked at that barbecue restaurant: I stole some food. It was a common practice of other employees. The manager I worked for even told me I should take some home with me. The owner was hard to work for because he had what most people considered to be a really abrasive personality. He often spoke very harshly to his employees. In all, however, I got along well with him.

When I hired on as a trainee, I was making a salary of $400 a month. I told my employer I would start for that but I could not support my soon-to-be family of three on that. He said as soon as I showed him I could do the job he would give me a raise. He told me the job required forty to forty-five hours per week; I told him that I was not willing to work Sundays, for personal reasons. He said that was fine.

The job turned out to be fifty to fifty-five hours per week. Even though I had received a $25 raise, I brought it to my boss' attention that I was having to work more hours than he had told me I would be working. He gave me another raise to $450 per month. The hours, however, remained the same.

I began to feel that the owner had not been honest with me and that he was taking advantage of me. Each week, I watched other managers take home what would amount to a feast for us. Finally, I reached the point of rationalizing that my boss owed me, so I took home a whole brisket and a couple of slabs of ribs one Friday. We had a couple over for dinner. They knew us well enough to know that we normally did not have money for a meal like that. As we sat down to eat, the guy asked how we could afford such a spread. I told him I had taken it because I had been working a lot of extra hours without getting paid for them. It was our custom to say a blessing before beginning to eat. He said, "It just ain't right to say grace over stolen food," and began eating without further ado.

I was so deeply convicted by his statement that the next day when I went to work, I took $25 (which we could not afford) and rang up sales for the food I had taken and put the money in the register.

The irony of the guy's comment didn't strike me until afterward, when I recalled how he got started in his business. He worked on new home construction. When he had been stationed in Vietnam, the requisitions officer at his base told him and some other guys that he had excess money in his budget. The officer told them that if he did not spend the rest of the money, his budget would be cut for the next year. So they all used the money for themselves to order stuff they could get really cheap over there. In addition to various electronics, my guest had acquired about $2,500 worth of power tools and had them shipped home, all at Uncle Sam's expense. Those tools enabled him to go to work when he got out of the service. As far I was concerned, every time his family sat down at the table and said grace, they were saying it over stolen food.

Even so, his remark helped me chart a more honest course for myself, one that has served me well many times when I have been tempted to depart from that path. In the short run, I was able to stand up to my boss when he told me I would have to work Sundays. I reminded him that part of our deal when I hired on had been that I would not have to work Sundays. He told me I would be replaced if I refused and I said I understood. He later backed down and even raised me to $550 per month when the manager quit.

In the long run, I figure I will have enough to account for to my Maker for my own actions without worrying about someone else's deeds.

Three Simple Secrets for Success in College

After our first child was born, I re-enrolled in college at the University of North Texas (UNT) to try to finish my degree. I changed majors twice more before I settled on psychology. When I started taking college classes again, I resolved to do three simple things: I would sit on the front row of class so I could hear to take the best notes possible; I would read the assigned material before each class so I could ask intelligent questions in class; and I would attend every class. It is sad to say, but doing these three things was sufficient to set me apart from the majority of the other students. I scored at the top of my classes and carried a 3.85 grade point average (GPA) on my last 60+ hours, compared to a 2.0 from my two and a half years at Austin College. Since UNT only considered the classes taken there in figuring the GPA, I miraculously graduated *magna cum laude..*

Memorable Quotes

One of the highlights of being at UNT was taking a class called "The Psychology of Personality" under Dr. Holloway. He sparked my interest in psychology. In a very great way, he is responsible for my completing my undergraduate degree. He made the subject come alive for me.

I still remember two memorable quotes from that class. One of Dr. Holloway's quotes was his definition of motivation. He said, "Motivation is being in a strange building and having a full bladder." But, my favorite quote was: "The reason that some people are in mental hospitals and we are not is that there are more of us." That helped me keep my whole academic experience in perspective.

A Cow Nose Best

One of my friends attended law school at the University of Texas in Austin. He related this story of a party his fraternity had at Lake Travis, a beautiful lake set in the rustic, heavily wooded hill country outside of Austin. At that time in the late sixties, it was not too developed. Other than sharing the site with some cattle, they had it to themselves. They had the usual kegs of beer, barbecue grills and picnic stuff. The party eventually reached the point where couples started wandering or driving off into the surrounding woods for some privacy. All of a sudden, a girl began shrieking hysterically and calling for help.

Alarmed, the others began homing in on her distressed cries. Several of them converged on a car, which seemed to be the source of the screams. They recognized it as belonging to one of their fraternity brothers.

As it turned out, the couple had disrobed and had climbed in the back seat of the car. The windows were down. They were so amorously engaged, with the lad on top of the girl, that they did not notice the approach of a curious cow. Apparently, the guy was so startled when the cow's wet nose poked him in his bare behind that he shouted and jumped up so hard that he hit his head on the roof of the car and knocked himself out, then fell on top of his girlfriend. She was so frightened—by his sudden outburst and collapse on her, as well as the cow sticking its head in through the back window of the car—that she went into hysterics. The guys had to pull him off of her and out of the car to revive him while the other gals helped restore her to a state of modesty.

I have extracted the following lesson from my friend's tale: Couples who park in cow pastures should leave their car windows up.

How a Creme Puff Changed My Life

College was a hotbed of pranks and dares. Sometimes they come back to haunt you later.

One night a bunch of guys were going to go out beer drinking. There was a guy, Duane, whom our fraternity was rushing. He showed up in the cafeteria that evening with two babes none of us knew. Don't ask me where the idea came from. One of the guys picked up a creme puff from his dessert plate and said, "Who will go in with me to buy Saunders' beer tonight if he smashes this creme puff over Duane's head?" They all said they were in.

So I calmly picked up the creme puff, walked over to their table and proceeded to slap it down on his head. A long stream of creme filling spurted onto the chest of one of the girls (who turned out to be his date), while several others ran down over his head and face, dripping onto his clothes. He didn't say anything; he just stood up, took his tray to turn in and then he and the girls left.

It's a bad sign when someone is so upset they don't say anything at all. I felt pretty bad about it; but, at the prospect of having my buddies pay for my beer, I did not let my conscience linger on any guilt too long. Ironically, when the carloads left for that evening's activities, each thought I was in the other car and left without me. I ended up stuck at the dorm that evening and partook of no beer. Duane, by the way, did not join our fraternity.

The real irony did not occur until nearly ten years later. I was in Houston interviewing for a job. I was sitting in the lobby of an insurance company, waiting to see the director of personnel about an underwriter position. Out walked Duane—he was the person in charge of hiring! During the interview, we managed to exchange a few pleasantries about our old college days. Each of us shared some news about some of our former classmates. Nothing was ever said about the creme puff.

I did not get the job. (I can't help but wonder how my life would have turned out if I had.)

The Original Language of the Holy Spirit

I attended Austin Presbyterian Theological Seminary after college and eventually earned a Master of Divinity degree. The academic challenges there were great. One of my favorite professors, Dr. Alsup, was lecturing on New Testament Greek. He had recently returned from Munich, Germany, where he had completed theological studies. He had been an official interpreter for the Munich Olympic Games. At times, we could tell he was lecturing from notes or materials that were in German.

Frustrations ran high in the rigorous academic environment at the seminary. I guess one of my classmates, Ernie, was particularly stressed one day. Dr. Alsup was reading a lengthy quotation on the inspiration of scripture, translating from German to English as he went. He was saying something like "in the original language as inspired by the Holy Spirit…" At that point, Ernie unintentionally blurted out his thoughts, saying, "What language was that, German?"

There was a sound like a rushing wind, but it was not the Holy Spirit. It was caused by the sudden collective intake of air by the entire class. There was not a single chuckle. Everyone held his or her breath. The fellow's face took on a look of sheer terror as he realized that he had just spoken out loud. The professor paused, looked up from the text for what seemed an interminably long time and then, without comment, returned to his reading as if nothing had happened. It was a long time before anyone exhaled.

No Reason to Wake Up

After seminary, I spent four months in a hospital chaplaincy intern program. I was assigned to the surgical intensive care unit. There were many heart-wrenching moments there, but none more so than the story of Ruth, an 88-year-old woman. Her legs had grown dark due to her failing circulatory system. Her doctor told her family and her that her legs were dangerously close to developing gangrene; if that happened and they did not remove her legs, she would die. She said she understood and told all of them that under no circumstances were they to amputate. She told them that she had lived a good, full life and that she did not want to end it as an amputee.

Ruth developed complications that left her comatose. Her doctor told them that unless both of her legs were immediately amputated, she would die. He pleaded with her family to consent to an operation. In spite of her clear wishes to the contrary, consent was given and the operation was performed.

Well, Ruth survived the surgery and made it through recovery. There was just one problem. She would not wake up. She was not in a coma. The staff was sure that she was conscious; she simply refused to open her eyes. She was physically capable of resuming her own care but she refused to respond. She had to be fed, cleaned and have all of her personal needs tended to. The staff asked for a chaplain to visit her.

I was sent to visit Ruth. What did they think a chaplain was supposed to be able to do? One of the nurses explained to me the background as I have described it above. Upon entering her room, the nurse introduced me to Ruth as though she were awake and listening. This would have been a perfect time for an angel to have appeared, but, to my knowledge, none did. Nothing miraculous happened. She never showed any signs that she was aware of my presence. I spoke to her for awhile. I told her I understood that she must be very angry. Then, I asked her if it was all right if I sat with her awhile, which I did while holding her hand. Finally, I told her that I did not know what she wanted or expected and that I certainly did not know what to say. So, I simply told her that I wanted to pray with her. I said a brief prayer and left. I do not know what happened to her after that, because she was released to a nursing care facility.

What makes people do things like her doctor and family did? Good intentions? I am sure they had them. It seems to me though, notwithstanding the best of intentions, that their disregard of her plain wishes was incredibly selfish. Perhaps I do not even have the right to question it, but, Ruth's story is one of those things I would like to ask my Maker about one day.

Law Professor Throws Down the Gauntlet

When I started law school, one of the first things I did was to go introduce myself to my faculty adviser, whom I shall call Dr. Wise. He was seated behind the desk in his office with half-lens reading glasses perched down on his nose. After looking at my file, he looked up over his glasses and said in what seemed to me like a condescending tone, "Mr. Saunders, I see you graduated from a seminary."

"Yes, sir," I answered.

He continued, "I have had two other students before who came to law school after seminary. They did not graduate, and I doubt you will, either."

I was stunned at this summary judgment. He went on to explain that he figured people who studied for the ministry were too empathetic and caring, where he believed law required one to be cold and dispassionate.

When the day came that I had finished my last final exam and I knew I had passed, I headed for Dr. Wise's office. I knocked on the door and, when he said to come in, I stuck my head in the door. I said, "Dr. Wise, I just wanted you to know that I am going to graduate." He looked at me with a quizzical expression on his face. I knew he did not not remember the gauntlet of challenge he had thrown down for me, but I did.

It was a tradition to ring a large bell on the first floor upon taking our last law school exam. Feeling satisfied, I left his office and headed for the bell. Looking back, his prediction of failure made me determined to show him. Dr. Wise may just have been responsible for my making it through law school.

PART 4:

MARRIAGE, IN-LAWS & KIDS

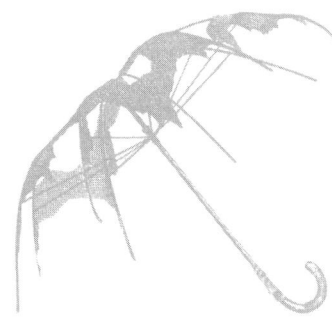

P.B. Doesn't Stand for Peanut Butter

A law school classmate of mine, Tony, had two small boys; his older son, whom I shall call Roy, was about four and a half at the time. My friend had taken him to see the movie, *ET*. Unbeknownst to Tony or his wife, Roy picked up a phrase that young Elliott called his brother in the early scene where the family was sitting around the table together. Tony's parents-in-law came to stay with them for a visit. His in-laws were very straight-laced and strict members of the Church of Christ.

So, you can imagine the raised eyebrows around the dinner table when Roy, in response to being corrected by his grandmother, retorted (quoting Elliott), "Shut up, penis breath!"

I have often heard it said that timing is everything. In this case, I would definitely have to agree.

"Oh, God," Parts 1 and 2

[The words "Oh, God" can be a prayer or an epithet or simply an expression of awe. The following vignettes illustrate how they can be all three at once.]

Part 1: We were driving from Austin to visit our families in Denton. My mother's elderly sister, a dear, saintly lady was travelling with us to visit my mom. As we were passing through Fort Worth, a car suddenly cut over in front of us from the right. I barely was able to react in time. I pulled sharply to the left. The car missed us by literally three or four inches at the most. I missed the concrete divider to our left by no more than the same margin. In the same instant I drew in a breath and stifled the words I was about to utter.

Rachel, my three-year-old, piped up in her sweet little voice, "Goddammit," which was exactly what I was going to say. I am sure she read it in my body language. Reflexively, I slapped her on the leg and said sternly, "No, we don't talk like that!" She looked up at me with those beautiful hazel eyes, big tears welling up in them, and in a quivering voice said, "Da Da, you hurt me." (All of this in front of my aunt.)

There was no mistaking where she had learned to say that. My heart broke as I looked into those innocent eyes and heard the pain in her voice. I felt no larger than a flea. (*"Oh God, if I could just take that back!"*) Of course, I had to tell her that Da Da was wrong and that I was sorry. I think the greatest lessons in humility I have experienced have been those I have had with my children.

Part 2: Shortly after the incident above, Rachel, her mom and I went shopping at a mall near our home. We went into a jewelry store to look in a case. The salesman was amazed at how well Rachel talked and had quite a conversation with her. At one point, he said, "You are a cute little girl. I bet you have lots of boyfriends, don't you?" She promptly replied, "Nope, just my dad." Did my heart ever swell. (*"Oh God, what did I do to deserve such love? Thank you!"*)

Cows Do Big Jobs

On the same trip home, we had a family picnic at some farm property my parents owned. My aunt, my daughter Rachel and I were walking around the edge of a lake. Rachel was wearing her cute, white Stride Rite sandals. Before I could stop her, she stepped in a very large, fresh cow patty.

With a squishing sound, her foot sank in as the stuff oozed in between her toes. She wrinkled up her nose at the feeling of it, looked up at me and said, "Oooh, Da Da, what was that?" Thinking quickly, I used the term my aunt had taught her to use to refer to doing a "number two" in the toilet, and said, "That is where a cow did a 'job'."

She looked down at it and then back at me with wide eyes. "Cows do BIG jobs don't they?" she said.

"Yes, they do," was all I could say as I lifted her out of it and stepped to the edge of the water to begin washing foot and sandal in the lake. Wouldn't it be nice if we could learn as easily which missteps to avoid in matters of the heart?

A "Hunger Banquet"?

Sometimes—well, actually, many times—churches do things that are well-intentioned but just are not clearly thought out. Barbie and I joined a church in San Antonio that had very active mission programs. Though there were fewer than 200 members, the giving in support of various church missions was the highest per capita of any church in the area. Our elders (church leaders) decided we needed to have a program to increase the congregation's awareness of world hunger. The program was scheduled for an upcoming fellowship dinner and was announced in the church newsletter as "Hunger Banquet." I don't know if anyone else saw the irony in that designation.

They decided to serve everyone plain rice, and nothing else except tea or coffee, in order to demonstrate what people in Third World countries had to eat. Each person was to get three cups of steamed rice (we were told that was the amount many people in poor countries had once every three days). To compound the irony, the woman who volunteered to fix the meal decided she just could not serve everyone plain rice. So, when dinner was served, it was discovered that she had added peas, carrots and chicken to the rice.

I thought the whole situation was incredible and said so to some folks around us. My daughter, Rachel, (who was now about five and a half years old and who ate three nutritious meals a day) had already polished off her plate and piped up, "Daddy, I want more!" There is nothing like a "hunger banquet" to drive home awareness of world hunger!

A Mosquito and a Willful Child

One night shortly before 9:00, I received a call at my work from my wife. She asked me to please come right home and deal with our younger daughter, Kierstin, who was three at the time. Barbie was at the end of her patience. It seemed that she could not get Kierstin to stay in bed and go to sleep. We were just closing up the department store where I worked, so I told her I would deal with it when I got home in about half an hour.

When I arrived at home, my wife told me that there had been a mosquito in our daughter's room and it had buzzed in her ear after the light had been turned out. Kierstin got out of bed and went to tell her mom. My wife went back into her bedroom but could not find the mosquito. She turned the light off again and left. Kierstin was right back a moment later insisting that the mosquito was still there. Barbie could still find no mosquito and told her not to get out of bed again or she would be in trouble. Kierstin was back a moment later saying she could not go to sleep in there. She put her back to bed once again and said she would get daddy's belt and spank her with it if she got out of her bed again. Kierstin told her to go get the belt, because she was going to get right back out as soon as her momma walked out. That was the point I at which I got the call.

I told Kierstin to come with me. We stopped in the kitchen and I got a can of insect repellent from the cabinet beneath the sink. We went into her room and I told her that I was going to spray it in the air. I explained to her that if the mosquito was still there, the spray would kill it and any other mosquitoes. I gave it about three or four good sprays. We got a nasty taste in our mouths, and I told her we could taste it because it was spreading all through the air in her room. I assured her that the mosquito was dead. Still spitting at the bitter taste, Kierstin climbed into bed. She was sound asleep in a couple of minutes.

I thought I was pretty clever handling the problem like that. My wife did not seem particularly appreciative of my solution. It doesn't matter what you do, sometimes you just can't win. Thereafter, whenever I reminded Barbie about the incident (which I felt a kind of perverse urge to do once in awhile), she would give me an annoyed look.

A big, biG, bIG, BIG Butt

When Kierstin, was six, I took her with me to the public library. They had turnstiles at the entrance and exit. As we were leaving, we were following a very large woman who got wedged in the turnstile. With some effort, the lady turned sideways and squeezed through. Kierstin, taking in the whole scene, extended the index finger of her right hand and poked the woman in the rear, exclaiming loudly, "Look, Da Da, that lady has a big, biG, bIG, BIG butt!" The woman glared at me. With my ears lit up like Rudolph's nose, I gave her my best chagrined look.

I did not want to embarrass my daughter by correcting her in front of the lady. When we got into our car, I told Kierstin that I knew she she was not trying to be mean. I explained to her that, even though it was the truth, saying something about the lady's size might have hurt her feelings. There are so many lessons to teach our children, and somehow they always find a way to remind us in public of the ones that we have not taught them yet.

If Santa Claus Is Not Real, What About God?

After Christmas of 1983, we were driving home to Houston from Denton. Kierstin was still six. She began an explanation as to why she did not think there was a Santa Claus. Different Santas she had seen had different voices; how could Santa be at different stores at the same time? They had fake beards; there were too many children in the world for Santa to make it to each one's house in one night; etc.

I thought: *Dear God, why did she have to pick this moment to be so perceptive? Can't she just be a child and enjoy Santa a little longer?*
I figured it would be her sister (age 9) who would have decided there was no Santa. Rachel questioned whether or not he was real; other kids at her school said he wasn't, that Santa was really her parents. I told her that Santa could not come and leave presents if she did not believe in him. I could tell she was running that through her brain. Apparently, she decided it wouldn't hurt to believe in Santa one more Christmas.

While I was still trying to decide how to answer Kierstin's question, she said, "What about God? Is He real?"

Oh thanks, Lord! That really helps, I thought sarcastically. In the flash of a synapse, I decided I had to tell her about Santa in order to be able to answer the last question. I told her that people made up

Santa Claus to represent the spirit of Christmas. Parents wanted Christmas to be fun and exciting for their children and Santa added to that. I went on to tell her that she was right; the Santas in the stores were people dressed in costumes.

"Now, God; that is a different matter. God is real." She was waiting for that. Kierstin immediately asked, "Well, if God is real, then why can't we see Him? Why can't we hear Him?"

Those were very good questions. Dang! *Come on Lord, a little help here would be appreciated. How do I answer my precocious six-year-old? It would be nice if I could hear You right now.*

I told her: "Well, I don't know why He doesn't let us see Him or hear Him; but, I believe with all my heart that He is real. Sometimes, when I think back about things that have happened, I feel that God was guiding me. I believe He is real and that He hears me when I talk to him. Some day, you will have to decide what you believe about God for yourself."

Then I told God: *Okay, Lord, I told her from my heart what I believe—the rest is up to You. From the time she was born, I have acknowledged Your claim upon her as a child of the covenant. I will continue to do so until the day she accepts Your claim for herself.*

I think raising children may be the truest test there is of a parent's faith in God.

You Have to Be Careful When You Handle a Gun

My father-in-law, Ted, was giving his son, Brian, who was ten at the time, a lesson in how to handle his CO_2 pistol. The pistol was supposedly jammed and Brian was watching while Ted explained what to do. I do not know whether Ted could not get the right grip on the gun or if he was just inadvertently holding it with his left index fingertip over the end of the barrel. Just as he was saying, "Son, you have to be careful when you are handling a gun," *Thoommp!* The gun discharged. He looked up in obvious pain and then down at his finger. At the sight of his own blood, he turned pale and dropped back into his armchair. He had to go to the doctor and have a BB removed from the bone in his finger. I will have to say this: it was one heck of a lesson. Brian has handled guns with the utmost respect ever since.

A Knothead and Nunchakus

There was constant friction between my two brothers-in-law. At the time of this incident, the older one, Dennis, was in his thirties; he was a military veteran and businessman. The younger one, Brian, was nineteen. Dennis was always on Brian's back about something, and Brian was always going out of his way to irritate the snot out of Dennis.

One day, the family was gathered at the home of Barbie's parents. Brian's car was parked in the driveway and Dennis saw a pair of nunchakus in the back seat. Nunchakus are a martial arts weapon consisting of two foot-long heavy sticks joined together by a rope or chain of about the same length. He reached in, grabbed one of the wooden sticks and began twirling the other stick around. The nunchakus were making a whirring sound like a fan blade.

Brian had been accepted to attend police academy. Dennis, in a superior tone of voice, started telling Brian that if they caught him with them, he would be kicked out of his class (since they are illegal to carry). Dennis was so into his lecture that he did not notice that the angle of the whirring nunchakus was progressively inclining closer and closer to his head. *Crack!* He hit himself. It sounded like someone had just split a coconut open with a hammer. Dennis' eyes crossed.

He dropped to his knees. God, that had to have hurt! Brian and I laughed so hard we both ended up collapsed on the driveway with tears streaming down our cheeks. (What is it about another person's pain that is so funny?)

Moral: If you act like a knothead with nunchakus, you will end up with one.

The Lady Magnet and the Mustard Mustache

Mitch, my next-door neighbor's brother-in-law, was one of those amazing (or disgusting, depending on how you looked at it) guys who attracted women like magic. He was a real lady magnet. No matter where he went, females hit on him. He never went out to a club that he did not take home his pick of the girls. He had the "stuff" and he knew it.

One day at a Whataburger restaurant, he was having lunch with some of his buddies. A group of girls were seated at another booth. "Hey," one of his friends said, poking him, "look, that chick is checking you out." Mitch looked up from a bite and, sure enough, one of the females was staring at him. She smiled. He smiled back. Keeping her eyes on him, she elbowed one of her companions and pointed to him while whispering something. The girlfriend, too, smiled; he grinned back, eating up the adoration. Both girls grinned at him. He turned to his pal, feeling very smug, and said, "I think they both got the hots for me."

His friend, laughing, handed him a napkin and said, "Wipe that [stuff] off your face, man." He wiped it across his mouth and looked at the napkin to see a big blot of mustard on it.

I guess chicks just can't resist a good-looking man with a mustard mustache.

A Rock Up the Nose and Smashed "Jack-o-laters"

My sister, Gail, and her son, Nick, were having dinner with my parents one evening. He was in first grade at the time. Suddenly Nick sneezed. There was a loud *"chink"* sound. Everyone stopped in mid-bite and looked to see what had happened. Gail asked, "Nick, what was that?"

"Oh nothing, Mom, just the rock I put up my nose at school today." It had been lodged there all day and he had not said anything about it. Kids!

My favorite story to tell on him, though, is from the time I visited them at their home in Dallas right before Halloween. Nick was a couple months shy of turning three. I arrived to find bits of pumpkin scattered all over their front porch and sidewalk. When they answered the door, I asked what had happened. He said, "Uncle Charlie, they smashed my jack-o-laters!"

I looked at his mom with a raised eyebrow and said, "Jack-o-laters?" She grinned and said, "Yeah, jack-o-laters." We both laughed.

Sorry, Nick, I just could not pass it up. I will probably have to tell that again to your kids one day.

PART 5:

LEGAL STORIES

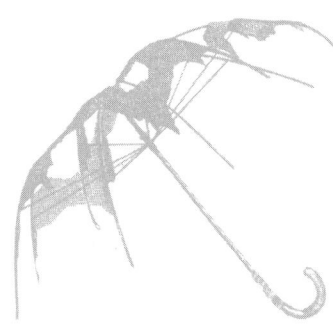

Pantyhose and Final Argument

It was mid-afternoon of the second day of a DWI trial. I was representing the accused. Both the State and Defense had finished their presentations of testimony in the case. It was time to begin final arguments to the jury. After a fifteen-minute recess, the jury was brought back into the courtroom and seated. The judge recognized the State. The lady prosecutor, who had rushed back into the courtroom right ahead of the jury, got up and began addressing the jurors. Evidently she had visited the ladies' room during the recess. She was parading back and forth in front of the jury box with the back of her dress gathered up in the top of her pantyhose, leaving her rear completely exposed. The jurors were trying to stifle smirks.

The bailiff, a seasoned deputy who had been around the courthouse for many years, got up from his desk and walked up behind her. She did not realize he was there. Was she ever startled when he reached out, grabbed hold of her dress and yanked it out, saying, "Pull your dress out of your panties, darlin'." Laughter erupted everywhere in the courtroom. Naturally, she looked mortified. To her credit, though, she went right ahead with her argument. The jury evidently was able to see the "bottomline" of the State's case and found the defendant guilty.

"If I'm Lyin', I'm Dyin'!"

There was a case involving grandparents seeking to get custody of their grandchild from their son. The grandfather had been on the witness stand for about an hour undergoing tough cross-examination by the son's attorney when this incident occurred. The attorney was trying to challenge the grandfather's truthfulness. The attorney asked the grandfather if he was sure of his answer to the last question, to which the man retorted, "If I'm lying, I hope that I do not leave this courtroom alive."

Mere seconds later, the witness clutched at his chest and said that he thought he was "going" [dying] right then. It took everyone a moment to realize that there really was something drastically wrong with the man. The Judge told the bailiff to call paramedics.

The man was dead by the time the paramedics arrived only minutes later. The jury was dismissed. Though some present thought it was a terrible coincidence, there were several who believed that a higher authority had been heard from. It certainly makes you think about swearing that oath when you take the witness stand, doesn't it?

The First Rule of Trial Law

Probably the first fundamental rule of trial law an attorney learns in law school is "Never ask a witness on the stand a question to which you do not already know the answer." I learned first-hand the importance of this rule early in my law practice.

One of the first cases I was assigned was to represent a lady who was the subject of a mental illness commitment proceeding. She was alleged to have tried to stab her husband with a steak knife. She seemed lucid when I spoke with her before her hearing. Before the lady could be committed to a mental hospital, there had to be, among other things, a finding that she was a danger to others or to herself. The only thing indicating that she might be a danger was the incident with the knife. Usually, these hearings were mostly a formality. It occurred to me that she might have an arguable defense if the medication she was taking meant she was no longer a danger, so, I called her to testify. It was a fatal error.

I asked her the following question, to which I did not know the answer: "Besides the incident where you tried to stab your husband with the steak knife, you have never done anything else to try to harm him, have you?"

She replied sweetly, "Other than the time I put the rat poison in his coffee, no."

I looked out of the corner of my eye at the judge. He raised one eyebrow as our eyes met; I noticed that he was already signing the commitment order.

Lawyer Bashing

There was another mental illness commitment case that is worthy of mention. I represented a fellow who seemed perfectly normal when I talked to him, until it came to the reason we were at court. He had been committed temporarily and the State was seeking to have him committed indefinitely in order to send him to a different mental health facility.

I asked him about the incident that led to these further commitment proceedings: He supposedly had attacked two hospital orderlies without any provocation. He told me they were walking toward him down the hall when he saw that they had "giant fly eyes." Since they were monsters, he attacked and started hitting them. He saw nothing unusual with his reason for attacking them and told me that if I had seen their eyes, I would have done the same thing. I thought to myself, "O . . . kay."

He insisted on having a trial. His family members, who meant well, said they could handle him and he posed no threat to them. I argued his family's position to the jury. They quickly returned a verdict. We sat at counsel table facing the judge, my client seated to my left. The prosecutors sat at a table to my right and the jury box was to the right of the prosecutors. The judge read the verdict that my client was to be committed.

I was looking straight ahead when suddenly it seemed that a gun burst went off right beside me. I never saw it coming, but my client had suddenly cocked his right arm and jabbed straight out, punching me directly over my left ear. The blow knocked me completely out of my chair. I shouted, "Shit!" before I realized it. By the time I got onto my feet, the two transport deputies who had been seated immediately behind us had my client's chair pulled over backwards. He was quickly subdued and they snapped handcuffs shut on him.

The judge excused the jury, and they all threaded single file between the counsel tables and the judge's bench (with their backs to the judge and eyes on the two deputies who had my client pinned and cuffed). Their eyes were locked on my client until they passed our table.

My client apologized; he said it just happened before he realized what he was doing because he was so upset. I told him that it was okay as the deputies led him away. But I had a hearing loss in my ear and it hurt for about two weeks.

I thought to myself; "You know, maybe the quality of our legal system would improve if attorneys had losing verdicts taken out of their hides." It would give a whole new meaning to "lawyer bashing."

Little Lady Lawyer from Dallas

The first time I ever walked into a courtroom on business as a lawyer was to get a judge to sign an agreed order in a case. The judge had been a brilliant—and notorious—trial lawyer in Denton County who took the bench after he retired. He had his flaws as a judge.

That day, he had a captive audience of five lawyers standing before him. He was telling stories from his days in the Marines. I don't know how long he had regaled the attorneys, but I overheard about 45 minutes of it.

Finally, he paused. It was not clear whether he had finished his story or if he was merely collecting his thoughts. At that point, a woman standing before him tried to be tactful and asked, "Pardon me, your honor, but with regard to the Court's order, will the Court be drawing it up or would you prefer that I prepare one for the Court to sign?" (It was a perfectly reasonable question to ask.)

He leaned forward, and looked at her over his half-focals. He said, "Listen here, little lady lawyer from Dallas: If there are two ways to do something and one is more trouble for the Court and the other is more trouble for you, which way do you think I am going to have it done?"

Ohhhh! You could feel the heat of her anger and humiliation radiate off of her, even at the back of the courtroom where I was standing. I thought to myself, "Oh my God, they never prepared us for this in law school." But she was a model of self-control.

Many lawyers would have found themselves in contempt before they even realized that any words had left their mouths. She was still red-faced when she left the courtroom about ten minutes later.

The legal profession was one of the last male chauvinist bastions to fall. In a large part, the solution to such attitudes has simply been attrition; that judge, like so many others of his era, has passed on. I am glad to say that much progress has been made since that first trip of mine into a courtroom.

The Definition of Coercive Contempt

That same judge was presiding over a case in which a woman was seeking to hold her ex-husband in contempt for failing to pay child support. In such cases, there are two kinds of contempt: punitive and coercive. The first kind allows a judge to jail someone for up to six months for each violation of an order of the court. The second kind allows the judge to jail someone indefinitely until they comply with an order of the court where the person willfully refuses to obey. The guy apparently responded to a question the judge asked him by saying, "I ain't paying her one red cent and you can't make me." The judge ordered the man to be put in jail for coercive contempt until he had paid all of his back child support, which amounted to several thousands of dollars.

I was in the judge's chambers [office] one day when he received a phone call. The judge said, "I don't know, I am only going to be in office for two more years." It turns out that the phone call was from the jail from that same man. He had been in there for five months and wanted to know when the judge was going to let him out.

I heard that the man was released after spending more than a year in jail when his family finally raised enough money to pay off his back child support.

The Volatile Judge

There was a judge who was known for his unpredictable temperament and volatile temper. Anything could set him off without warning. Lawyers who conducted trials in his court usually ended up with badly frazzled nerves. The judge's unexpected and frequent outbursts could wear down the patience of even the most experienced of attorneys.

On one occasion, a lawyer was trying to argue a point with the judge. The judge suddenly exploded, screaming: "Are you trying to show your contempt for this Court?" The lawyer instantly snapped back at the judge, "Your honor, I could not possibly show my contempt for this Court!"

The judge looked thoughtful for a moment. "That was a good one," he said, nodding at the lawyer. "All right, you may continue." They proceeded as though nothing had happened.

"Officer, I Don't Know This Guy"

My former brother-in-law, Brian, told me of this experience with the law. He had been to a party at a popular, all-you-can-eat fried catfish place up in Oklahoma (a little over an hour's drive away from Denton). When it was time to go home, he ended up riding with a fellow he did not know. The guy was obviously three sheets to the wind. As they crossed back over the border into Texas, they could see flashing red lights ahead where a Department of Public Safety (DPS) officer had a vehicle pulled over on the right side of the road. The driver pulled his car off of the highway and came to a stop behind the patrol car. He rolled his window down as the officer began walking cautiously back toward them.

The DPS officer asked, "What seems to be the problem, sir?"

The guy responded, with very slurred speech, "Oh, noshing izz the problem, Mr. Officer, sir. I am jush waiting for thish light to turn green so I can go."

The guy had no time to react before the officer pulled him out through the open window. At the same time, Brian climbed out of the passenger side and headed toward the front of the car. The patrolman asked him where he thought he was going.

Brian said, "I don't know this guy. I was just hitching a ride to Denton." The officer told him, "You better go on, then, and get out of here." Brian wasted no time hiking on down the highway!

Margaritas and a Blue Light Special

I am now married to Sarah. She has a friend who lives in Atlanta, Georgia, who told her the following story that she swears is true.

The lady had been out partying with friends. On her way home, she was stopped by a highway patrol officer. His vehicle had flashing blue overhead lights. He left them on while he approached her car. He asked her to exit the vehicle. She was unable to stand up without leaning on the side of the car. The cop asked her if she had been drinking.

She told him, "Hell, yeah, I've had like thirteen margaritas."

He said, "Ma'am, I am not even going to give you any sobriety tests. I am placing you under arrest for suspicion of driving under the influence."

She said, "You're a cop? Oh, thank goodness; for a moment, I thought I was in K-Mart."

PART 6:

MISCELLANEOUS

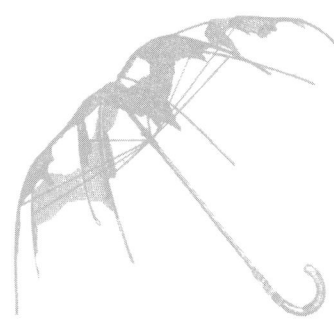

The Problem Runs In the Family

My friend Joe related this story to me. He attended the funeral of his father. After the church service, his family was getting ready to go to the cemetery. Joe held the door for his mother as she got into the front passenger seat of the limousine. Next, he held the door for her father to get in the car in the seat directly behind her.

As Joe walked around, to get in on the other side, he heard his grandfather ask, "Uh, who ... who is that young man? Don't I know him from somewhere? He looks familiar to me."

Joe's mom said, "Daddy, that is Perry Joe, your namesake, your oldest grandchild. You know who he is."

As he got into the car beside his granddad, Joe teasingly said, "Who ... who are you? Don't I know you from somewhere? You look real familiar to me."

His grandfather reached forward and tapped Joe's mother on the shoulder, and with complete earnestness said, "You know, he has the same problem I do."

Is God There If He Doesn't Seem to Answer Prayers?

I used to have zealous Christian friends who were involved in campus ministry organizations or churches that emphasized witnessing to other people. They used to try to talk to me about my personal beliefs. I do not know how many times different people handed me a little tract called, "The Four Spiritual Laws." (I once heard someone refer to it as "The Four Spiritual Flaws.") The main thrust of their inquiries was twofold: (1) Had I been saved? and (2) *When* had I been saved?

Having been raised in the church by my parents, I could never identify a magic moment when I was "saved." A friend named Phil (with whom I had many deep discussions about our beliefs and various scripture passages and whom I believed to be a very devout Christian) told me how to answer that question. It worked: Anytime someone asked me when I was saved, I simply said "When Jesus was crucified and then raised from the dead." You would be surprised how quickly that stops them.

This stage of my life involved deep searching of my soul. I often felt that I was utterly lost. I prayed for things in good conscience, but nothing seemed to happen in response to my petitions. My prayers finally were reduced to, "God, if You are there, then do something in my life that I will recognize as being unmistakably Your doing." It seemed that even these requests fell on deaf ears. I concluded that if a person with faith the size of a mustard seed could move mountains, then I must have none, since I could not get even the simplest of my prayers answered.

I reached such despair that one evening in my darkened house, I lay on the floor and wept. I felt that I was nothing, that I was completely lost. As I lay there, I cried out, "Father, help me." That is a prayer I know many others have prayed under similar feelings of utter despair. Strangely, in the days that followed, I felt better, even though I received no definite answer that I could discern.

This experience was tucked into the back of my mind when I went off to seminary, still searching for answers. Many books I read and preachers I heard emphasized that when a person became a Christian, they became filled with the Holy Spirit. It seemed that they were saying that the proof that a person had really received the Holy Spirit (thus, was a true Christian) was his or her experiencing the phenomenon known as speaking in tongues. I was very concerned because I had never had that experience.

A fellow seminary student named Jim had spoken in tongues. I shared my concern with him. Jim assured me (and I agreed with him after praying, thinking about it and reading various scripture passages) that if I was saved but had never spoken in tongues, then I must have another gift of the Spirit. He explained that there were different gifts of the Spirit and that each Christian received at least one. So, if I did not have the gift of speaking in tongues, which was the least of the gifts of the Spirit, then I must have received one the higher ones. Jim helped lift a great burden from my heart, and I owe him my thanks.

The final piece in my search came one evening as I sat in my car having another of those deep discussions with a classmate of mine, Paul. We were talking about my lingering concern over seemingly unanswered prayers. He asked me a classic philosophical question that I had encountered before in a college class called "The History of Psychology." Paul asked, "When a tree falls in the forest and there is no one there to hear it, does it make a sound?" I knew my own answer to that question was unequivocally "yes." Suddenly, it all fell into place.

What I am describing was an insight, not a physical sensation; but, the only words I have to express what I experienced is to say that though it was dark outside it seemed as if there was suddenly a bright light. Everything became clear in that instant and has never dimmed since. The only way I had been able to call out, "Father, help me," back in my time of despair was because God really exists and somehow communicated with my spirit. My spirit recognized something my conscious mind did not. Furthermore, I realized with full conviction that God exists whether or not I perceive an answer to any of my prayers (the same way I knew there was a sound in the forest even if no one was there to hear the tree fall). I also knew in that same instant that God had answered my deepest prayers to do something that was unmistakably His doing.

I do not recall the date, though curiously, I do remember that it was on a Wednesday. But from that day until the present, I can honestly say that I have had no doubts about my faith. I cannot foresee any circumstance that would cause me to doubt. Please understand that I say this with the deepest humility; I do not mean it to be in any way boasting. I pray that my faith will never be put to the test.

Many people find it hard to believe in a kind, loving God because of the bad things that happen in the world. It has been my observation that the Bible does not attempt to explain the origin of evil in the world or why bad things happen to good people. It simply states that, in spite of the existence of evil, people have experienced the goodness, mercy and grace of God like that of a loving father. It will be my belief as long as my physical shell retains life that God is good, that He has claimed me as His child and that I can and do trust Him.

I hope (I pray) that at least one person who reads my account above will find a key to his or her own questing for answers. To my other readers, I hope you did not find these ramblings too painful.

"The Greatest Single Fee I Have Ever Earned For My Professional Services"

I heard the following story at an Amway rally. I believe that the name of the gentleman that told the story was Curtis Ledbetter. (I do not know if he was the author of the story.)

There was a boy who was blind from either birth or very early childhood. His mother worked for low pay. She was ever vigilant to watch for articles on new medical research and procedures for blindness. She learned all about her son's condition. One day she read about a new operation that offered hope for precisely the kind of blindness he had. She contacted the doctor who had developed the surgical procedure. She arranged for her son to be seen. She received word that her son was an ideal candidate for the operation. She took in mending and cleaned jobs outside of her regular work. Still, it seemed that she would never be able to save enough to pay for his operation. People who knew of her goal helped raise money and finally the day came when she was able to schedule her son's operation.

When they checked him into the hospital, he had along with him his favorite teddy bear; it had been his constant companion since he was a baby. It was worn, missing one eye, one arm and one leg. But it was his special friend and he asked to be allowed to have it with him in his room. The surgeon came to see him the day before his operation to make sure everything was all right and to explain to the little boy about the operation. The doctor asked him if he had any questions. The little fellow had one: Could he have his teddy bear in the operating room with him? The physician told him that he could take it into surgery with him and that he would make sure the staff knew he was to have the teddy bear with him during the operation.

The procedure went fine. When he awoke from the anesthesia, the little boy was happy to find his teddy bear was there with him. Several days passed. Finally, the day came when they took off the last of his bandages. He could see. Upon seeing his mother for the first time, he said, "Mommy, you are even more beautiful than I imagined." They cried tears of joy.

A few days later, he was released from the hospital. When it was time for him to leave, they pushed him out in a wheelchair. The physician was there to see him off. The little boy said, "Thank you, doctor. I want you to have this," and held out his teddy bear. The man shook his head to say "no," but the boy's mother, who was standing behind her son, nodded that it was all right. Reluctantly, the doctor took the teddy bear.

When the little boy and his mother arrived home, there was a large package awaiting them that had been specially delivered. It was addressed to the boy. Inside was a large, brand-new teddy bear from the physician.

Meanwhile, back in the doctor's office, inside a glass dome, there soon sat a worn, one-eyed, one-armed, one-legged teddy bear. A brass plate on the base bore the inscription, "The greatest single fee I have ever earned for my professional services."

This story has always held special significance to me because of my father. He was a highly respected dentist for more than four decades. Dad confided in me that he viewed his work as providing people a service. He said that because of that he only charged what he believed to be a fair fee for his services instead of charging the much higher fees that dentists charged in Dallas. This influenced my own view of my work as an attorney. It is almost humorous the number of times someone has made the comment to me that, of course, they did not make the kind of money I made as an attorney. If only they knew.

"Feet Hurt! Boots Off!"

This, too, is a story I heard told at an Amway rally. The storyteller was a Diamond Direct distributor who lived in Dallas. I do not remember his name, but so far as I know, he is the author of the story.

He once worked on freight docks in Dallas. During the winter, the workers' feet would get very cold on the concrete docks no matter how thick the socks they wore. The speaker said he had received a pair of electric socks one Christmas. He wore them to work and was bragging on how warm his feet were going to be. The socks worked great and his feet were toasty for about two hours, but then the batteries ran down. No matter what kind of batteries he tried, they all lasted about two hours. He could not afford batteries at that rate.

He thought on the problem and a solution came to him. He got a military surplus flak jacket and cut holes inside the pockets. He then soldered some wires to the clips on the top of the electric socks. He ran those up the inside of his pants legs, out the waist and in though the jacket pockets. To the ends of the wires running into his pockets, he soldered alligator clips. He then set a twelve-volt battery inside each pocket. He was ready to impress the guys at the freight docks.

At work that night, when it got cold in the early hours of the morning, he told his co-workers to watch. He reached into his pockets and attached the alligator clips to the posts on the batteries. There was a flash and a puff of smoke from his boots. (At the rally, he asked the audience, "Have you ever hurt so bad that your brain goes into this kind of primitive mode?") All he could think was, *"Feet hurt! Boots off!"* He began tugging madly at the laces to get his boots off, never realizing that all he had to do was unhook the clips in his pocket.

Based on my childhood experience with electricity and his story, I have never had any desire to try electric socks.

What Do You Get When You Cross a Garden Club With a Gentlemen's Club?

Sometimes a prank backfires on the prankster (as my pencil-through-textbook experience proves); other times the prank takes an unforeseen twist that works out far better than could ever have been envisioned. This is a case of the latter.

A few years ago my father learned of the death of one of his cousins. The deceased cousin's family came up with a special way for their relatives to remember him. They took his many garden club scrapbooks and videotaped some forty years' worth of photos of him with various plants he had raised and awards he had received. This videocassette was then circulated among the relatives. Each person receiving it was to view the video and then forward it to the next name on the list.

The tape ran about an hour in length. Dad found it to be a bit dull and thought something was needed to liven it up. He remembered a video he had received from a friend as a gag gift, which featured the women of a well-known gentlemen's club in Houston, Texas. So he had the video of the strippers dubbed onto the end of his cousin's garden club videotape. Dad then sent it on to the next person on the list. A short time afterward, he received a letter from her husband.

The letter explained that when she had received the tape, she immediately stuck it in their VCR and tried to play it. It did not work. So she took the tape to a nearby Montgomery Ward store to see if it would play there. She figured that would be a simple way to determine if the problem was with the videotape or with her VCR. Her husband went with her.

Upon arriving in the video electronics department, she explained her problem to a salesman who was glad to help her. He put the videotape in one of their display machines. Instantly, rock and roll music blared while a close-up of a woman's bouncing breasts brightened thirty or more TV sets around the department. Her husband wrote that it was the first time he had seen her speechless in over fifty years of marriage. He would not have believed that her face could get any redder until the salesman asked if he could get a copy of the tape.

To this day, when we have family get-togethers and this story is recalled, Dad still laughs with an almost devilish kind of glee while Mom dons a disgusted frown.

The Cockroach Letter

When I was growing up, one of the most famous professional wrestlers was Fritz Von Erich, who lived in the nearby town of Grapevine, Texas. He was the guest speaker one noon before the Denton Kiwanis Club. My dad took me to hear him speak. I still remember a wonderful story that he told that day.

Fritz travelled extensively as a professional wrestler. He always flew on Braniff Airlines (which is no longer in business). He claimed that he flew more miles with Braniff than any other individual. One day, he discovered a cockroach on his food tray. He showed it to the flight attendant. She apologized profusely and brought him a new tray of food.

After thinking about it, Fritz decided that the airline probably would appreciate hearing from him about the incident since he was such a good customer. So, he wrote a letter to Braniff's president.

He received an immediate reply to his letter. Braniff's president had personally signed it and thanked Fritz for bringing the incident to his attention. He stated that he had fired the head stewardess; he also had the aircraft taken out of flight service and fully fumigated. The president apologized again, thanked him for his business and invited him to continue doing business with Braniff.

Fritz said that he was shocked that by the reaction. He felt that firing the head stewardess was extreme. As he folded the letter and started to slip it back into the envelope, he noticed a small piece of paper stuck inside the envelope. He pulled it out. It was a memo in the president's own handwriting to his secretary. It said, "Send this S.O.B. the Cockroach Letter."

One cannot help but wonder if this attitude of Braniff's president was one of the contributing factors to the airline's eventual failure. I seriously doubt that a business can long survive with such a callous view of its customers.

"Always Do What You Believe Is Right, Always!"

San Antonio is the home of Church's Fried Chicken. When we lived there, I decided to write its founder, Mr. George W. Church, Sr. I told him I was a young businessman just starting out and I wanted to know his story, how he got started and built such a successful business, and what advice he might give me.

I got back a letter a couple of weeks later on his letterhead and signed by him personally. It said, "Always do what you believe is right, always!"

I was indignant that he did not share his life story with me and that he blew me off with what I considered to be a flippant answer rather than giving me specific advice. I hate to admit this; I crumpled the letter up and threw it in the trash. Would I ever like to have it back! It would be framed on the wall over my desk.

I should have felt honored that he took the time to share that pearl of wisdom with me. Even though I no longer have the letter, I have never forgotten its message. When I have failed to do my best, it is usually because I did not follow Mr. Church's simple advice.

Ladies Found No Humor in Headline

When I was in junior high school, I think around my ninth grade year, our local newspaper incurred the wrath of several prominent ladies in the community. My mother's garden club was (and still is) named the Hoe and Hope Garden Club. They had a flower show. An article about the show appeared a day or two later in the newspaper. It bore the title, "Hoers Present Awards." The ladies found no humor in the headline. To say they were "hot" would be an understatement. I still chuckle when I recall it.

Hair Pieces and Hell

My wife, Sarah, contributed this one. She was raised in a Pentecostal Church. Her family lived in Tucumcari, New Mexico, at the time. They had a new, young preacher in training. One Sunday, he was thundering away about the sin of women wearing adornments. He railed that God did not intend for women to wear revealing clothing, jewelry, makeup, hair pieces, etc. These were all things worn by harlots. Women who adorned themselves with such could be sure that they were going straight to Hell.

In the middle of this tirade about wigs and hair pieces, he shouted, "Some of you women have more hair in your drawers than you do on your heads!" Sarah and her mother were just irreverent enough to find humor in this statement. The young minister went on, never realizing the possible connotation of his message.

Afterthought

The experiences, anecdotes and stories told in this collection have been shared with one goal in mind: to be refreshment for the heart. Whether a particular one made you laugh, cry, angry, think or simply reminisce or whether you agree or disagree with any of my observations or conclusions, it is my earnest wish that you feel that this book has in some way nourished you. To that end, thank you for honoring me with your reading of it.

In the event this little book is well received, I hope to follow it up with a second volume composed of readers' contributions. If you have a personal experience, an anecdote or a story that illustrates one of life's little lessons or that you feel is simply good for the heart and you would like to share it, please send it to me at the following address:

> Charles P. Saunders
> 1000 Sandpiper Dr.
> Denton, TX 76205

Please include your full name. If someone else is the author of your submission, please include the author's full name (if known). If your submission is used, credit will be given both for the submission and the authorship. Thank you.

ABOUT THE AUTHOR

CHARLES P. SAUNDERS is a native of Denton County, Texas. He earned a B.A. degree in psychology from North Texas State University (now the University of North Texas) in 1975, a M.Div. degree from Austin Presbyterian Theological Seminary in 1978, and a J.D. degree from South Texas College of Law in 1983. He retired from his law practice in Denton, Texas, after fifteen years and now is part owner of a comics and game store in Carrollton, Texas.

Charles has been blessed with two daughters, three grandchildren and three stepchildren. He is presently working on a fantasy fiction novel.